STARTING AT ZERO

STARTING
AT
ZERO

A GUIDE TO MAKING YOUR DREAMS COME
TRUE WHEN EVERYTHING ELSE IS F**KED

FREDDIE BENNETT

Matador
9 Priory Business Park,
Wistow Road, Kibworth Beauchamp,
Leicestershire. LE8 0RX
Tel: 0116 279 2299
Email: books@troubador.co.uk
Web: www.troubador.co.uk/matador
Twitter: @matadorbooks

ISBN 978 1 80046 114 7

British Library Cataloguing in Publication Data.
A catalogue record for this book is available from the British Library.

Printed and bound by CPI Group (UK) Ltd, Croydon, CR0 4YY
Typeset in 11pt Adobe Garamond Pro by Troubador Publishing Ltd, Leicester, UK

Matador is an imprint of Troubador Publishing Ltd

To Oli & Luke,
the most fantastic boys a father could ask for.
I will forever be in awe of you.

To Dad,
if only you could see me now.

Decide.
So, do it. Decide.
Is this the life
you want to live?
Is this the person
you want to love?
Is this the best you can be?
Can you be stronger?
Kinder? More compassionate?
Decide.
Breathe in.
Breathe out
and decide.

Meredith Grey

CONTENTS

ONE

TAKING THE LEAP

As the chasm stretched out before me, I felt the faint, warm trickle of piss running down the inside of my leg. It served as a reminder – not that I needed one – of the challenge in front of me. I knew there was little margin for error: if I got this wrong, it wasn't just my ego that would be severely damaged – I'd be facing serious injury.

Looking along the metallic zipline, taut and straining as tightly as my nerves, I wished there was someone to help me – an expert who could offer guidance, a tutorial video or an instruction manual – but there was none. The downside of attempting something no one had done before meant there wasn't exactly an abundance of experience or knowledge to call upon.

Nevertheless, as I took a breath to try to slow a heart that was beating like an over-revved engine, threatening to punch a hole through my chest, several pieces of advice were yelled at me from the watching crowd:

"*You need to jump as far as possible to clear the trees.*"

"*Make sure you cut your speed in the final few metres, otherwise you'll be sliced to shreds on the wire.*"

Or my personal favourite, "*I can't wait to see you fuck yourself up!*"

Blowing on my hands for what felt like the hundredth time, to try to clear the sweat that had blossomed on my palms, I allowed myself a quiet chuckle. It always seemed to be the people who were willing to *not* take the risk – who wanted nothing more than to sit back in their comfort zones and laugh while watching others try and fail – who offered the most advice.

Their words hit me like grenades, threatening to dislodge me from my platform 10 feet above the ground. It would be so easy to give up now, make an excuse – any excuse – and step away from the challenge. I could blame the weather, the imposing tree trunk I rested against, the equipment, etc. – or I could simply tell the truth and admit I was terrified.

It took all my strength to get a grip on the choking panic rising from the pit of my stomach and stuff it back deep down inside. Caught in that bewildering, mind-spinning zone – the tiny place where the concepts of *terror* and *possibility* overlap – I felt overwhelmed by what I was about to do. My mind was screaming to change course, with its primal urge of self-preservation pushing me towards the safe, familiar, controlled comforts of home. I wanted to obey these persuasions, but they were drowned out by a stronger urge – the absolute certainty that I *had* to do this.

This is more commonly known as an 'oh shit' moment.

There was no going back now.

I blew the air out of my lungs and peered down the straight line of wire that was cutting through the hazy summer's evening sunshine like a laser. This attempt had been the topic of discussion throughout the day. The truth be told, as soon as the concept of a zipline had been discussed, I knew that I would be the person stepping forward.

The zipline concept is beautiful in its simplicity. You find a point, be it on a structure, a canyon wall, a building or, in my case, a tree. Next, you find another point that is ideally slightly lower and in a direct line of sight from the first point. Finally, you attach a wire 'line' between these two spots and, hey presto, you have a zipline whereby people can whizz merrily downwards at the mercy of gravity before coming to a gentle halt at the end of the exhilarating journey.

I loved a zipline because it required so little thought. There was no technique to worry about, no manoeuvres to learn, and no intimidating phrases and/or acronyms that sound like a foreign language to anyone but the most seasoned pro. All I needed to do was to grab on to a small, handheld rig sitting either side of the wire and let myself go. Once someone started going along a zipline, they were guaranteed to experience a journey of pure, unbridled joy. As with so many things in life, the only challenge to overcome is to take that first leap away from safety and make sure our desire to experience something new outweighs our fears of the unknown.

And yet, no matter how hard I tried to recall every inspirational speech I had seen on a movie screen or imagine every motivational poster I had ever glanced at on a wall, the warm dribble seeping down my leg alerted me that it was time to take the leap. I couldn't back out now, and, besides, if I waited much longer, then a damp patch would start appearing on my grey jogging trousers. Although the zipline struck fear into me, nothing was more terrorising than the thought of embarrassing myself in front of the expectant audience that surrounded this new, untested challenge.

Murmurs began to vibrate through the crowd like a swarm of bees. Watches were checked, heavens were glanced at, and cheeks were puffed. I knew I had been dallying for too long. There was a real risk that the observers would get bored and leave. If no one was watching, would I still go through with it? *When a stupid idiot falls from a tree in a forest, and there is no one to see him fail, does he make a sound?*

Did I undertake these challenges in order to gain the acceptance and approval of others, or did I do it for myself? If I asked myself enough deep, hypothetical questions, would I still have to go through with it, or could I possibly talk myself out of this attempt?

It was now or never. I stepped forwards, inching my feet over the wooden ledge so the soles of my shoes peered straight down to the rocky ground, which was criss-crossed with emerald moss and scarred, exposed tree roots. Gripping the handles of the rig so tightly that my knuckles blazed white through the skin of my hands, I tentatively tested the load and tightness of the wire.

In my mind, I'd always imagined this moment differently. Perhaps I would make an inspirational speech to the crowd to get them on their feet and roaring their approval. Maybe I would count to three before soaring through the trees in slow motion, accompanied by a rousing operatic soundtrack in my ears.

The reality was somewhat different. I bounced on the balls of my feet, took a huge breath and started the countdown: "*Ten… nine… eight…* Oh fuck it, here goes nothing."

I didn't think NASA would be offering me a gig any time soon.

My decision to jump at that time was based on nothing but instinct. I knew I could only pause, observe, dwell and ponder for so long. On realising that there would never be a perfect time to make my move, I had decided to act.

Fortune favours the brave, I reminded myself as I felt the rush of air from the intense acceleration hitting my face. Not thinking, not worrying and with my mind suddenly clear of the everyday trivialities with which it was usually bombarded, I allowed myself a grin and anticipated the cheers from the crowd. I had done it: once again, I had escaped my comfort zone.

The sound of the snapping wire cut through the air like a whip, bringing me to my senses instantly. As time slowed down, I realised I had hardly commenced my zipline journey. The flimsy cable had surrendered as soon as it attempted to take my weight, and instead of a rapid but graceful descent, like a majestic swan landing on the mirrored surface of a lake, I was plummeting to earth like a pigeon that had just received some bad news from a shotgun.

Panicking, my arms spun outwards with my hands grasping for something, anything, that would break my fall. All the fear I had been pushing down inside me exploded from my mouth in a garbled, unintelligible wail. My left hand made contact with the dry, unyielding trunk of the tree, and my fingers scraped down the rough bark rapidly, like the nails of an evil teacher on a blackboard.

By some strange, centrifugal force of nature, I was drawn closer to the tree as I plummeted to the earth. Instinctively, I threw the nearest part of my body against the coarse wood in a feeble attempt to protect myself.

Unfortunately, that part of my body happened to be my face.

I closed my eyes and bit my tongue as I felt the left side of my forehead, eye socket, cheek and chin being eroded away as neatly and efficiently as if I had experienced a run-in with an industrial sanding machine. As my skull vibrated in time with the contours of the tree it was being polished against, all I could think was, *Why couldn't you have played it safe for once? Why couldn't you have just been one of the crowd?*

The ground prevented me from answering my own questions as the impact from the fall punched the last gasps of air from my lungs. Lying dazed on the floor, I watched the mixture of shock and enjoyment on the faces of the crowd. Some were genuinely concerned and worried I had sustained serious injuries. Others, I saw through my blurred and blood-splattered vision, were seemingly *happy*. Their pleasure was not caused by the display of putting my face through nature's most efficient cheese grater but because they believed they had been proved *right*. My majestic failure and my bruised and crimson body were all the proof these onlookers needed to vindicate their decision to play it safe. As far as they were concerned, they hadn't taken a leap of faith, turned away from facing their fears, stepped away from rejection and settled even deeper into their comfort zones. Now, they were patting themselves on the back and congratulating each other for never dipping their toes into the seas of their limitations.

There and then, I promised myself I would be different. It was in that raw moment of suffering that I decided to take a different path. Despite the embarrassment, the blood, the disfigurement and the pain, I had never felt more alive. I had seen a glimpse of what my body and mind would be willing to do if I allowed it to, and now I just wanted more.

However, my dreams and desires for stepping outside my comfort zone would have to wait, for, at that very moment, I had more pressing matters to attend to. I had to patch myself up and find a way to plug the deep, bleeding holes that ran down the left side of my face. Otherwise, I was going to look such a dick in front of my classmates at school on Monday.

TWO

IT'S ABOUT TIME

"It's not death that most people are afraid of. It's getting to the end of life only to realize that you never truly lived."

Prince Ea

It would be easy to say this book is about motivation. I could make you endless promises about how the words contained within these pages will turn your life around, encourage you to quit that job you hate, ask that person out, give you a body like that of the gods and the untouchable confidence of a crooked politician.

Plenty of what has already been said and written on personal development has been refreshed and regurgitated so much that it has become a cliché. We've faced our fears and done it anyway, leaned in, awakened the giant within and told the world that it can't hurt us. For some of us, the impact has been huge. People have turned their lives around and found the purpose and inner peace they had been searching for – or hiding from – for a lifetime. We know we must think clearer, act better, eat cleaner, love more, give more and appreciate more. In many cases, we've done this and made improvements to our lives.

But sometimes it feels that something is still, well, missing?

Given that the self-help industry will be worth $13.2 billion in the US alone by 2022,[1] isn't all the support people could ever need already out there? Around 19 million self-help books were purchased in the US in 2019,[2] and 3 million self-help books were purchased in the UK in 2018, which is a 20% rise from the previous year.[3] Every fear, phobia, anxiety, concern and mental conflict can be addressed through the support that already exists in the self-help market.

Despite all this, we are putting a sticking plaster on a dam. The most recent research from the Institute for Health Metrics Evaluation appears to show that in 2017 just under 300 million people worldwide suffered from anxiety, about 160 million experienced a major depressive disorder and another 100 million endured a milder form of depression.[4]

The common (and misleading) argument is that we have so little to be depressed about. Sure, COVID-19 has turned our world upside down and we are experiencing something of an economic and political crisis currently, but, overall – when you compare our lives to the Victorian era, the Middle Ages or the Stone Age – we've never had it so good.

Despite how it may feel, the developed world is getting increasingly comfortable. In the UK, before the pandemic hit, consumer spending was increasing by almost 4% each year, with the fastest growing spending categories being amusement parks, travel agents, bars and restaurants (but let's face it, that's not going to be happening again any

---

1   LaRosa, J. (2018). The $10 Billion Self-Improvement Market Adjusts to a New Generation. Market Research Blog. https://blog.marketresearch.com/the-10-billion-self-improvement-market-adjusts-to-new-generation

2   Anderson, P. (2020). NPD: 'A Decade of Personal Exploration' Ahead in US Self-Help Books. Publishing Perspectives. https://publishingperspectives.com/2020/01/npd-sees-decade-of-personal-exploration-opening-usa-self-help-books/

3   Walker, R. (2019). Stressed Brits buy record number of self-help books. *The Guardian*. https://www.theguardian.com/books/2019/mar/09/self-help-books-sstressed-brits-buy-record-number

4   Rice-Oxley, M. (2019). Mental illness: is there really a global epidemic? *The Guardian*. https://www.theguardian.com/society/2019/jun/03/mental-illness-is-there-really-a-global-epidemic

time soon).[5] It was a similar story across the pond, where spending in the US was increasing by between 2% and 3% annually in the last 20 years. Online sales for Black Friday in 2019 grew by 19.6% over the previous year.[6]

In fact, the numbers are only going in one direction. The European Commission reports, "By 2030, the global middle class is expected to reach 5.3 billion people. This means an additional more than 2 billion people with increased purchasing power than today." [7] And yes, this is still expected to be the case, once the damage caused by COVID-19 is resolved.

And let's be honest, is a larger, happier middle class *such* a bad thing? It's natural that we want comfort, especially after the devastation COVID-19 has caused. Why on earth would we seek more hardship? Times are tough right now, and so many of us feel like we are 'starting at zero'. However, we still have shelter, clean water, electricity and Netflix. We have lives that our ancestors assumed were solely the privilege of the gods, but it seems that so many of us are feeling more lost and unfulfilled than ever before.

Richer, more 'comfortable' countries seem to experience higher rates of anxiety in their population than poorer countries and – in a finding that surprised even the researchers – anxiety also interferes more with their people's lives, activities and responsibilities. The countries with the highest prevalent lifetime rates of generalised anxiety disorder (GAD) are Australia (8%), New Zealand (7.9%) and the US (7.8%). In comparison, the prevalence in Peru is 1.1% and in Nigeria is 0.1%.[8]

In the US – which is widely seen as one of the richest, most prosperous and most powerful countries in the world – anxiety

---

5   Armstong, M. (2019). *The UK's Fastest Growing Consumer Spending Categories.* Statista. https://www.statista.com/chart/18262/fastest-growing-consumer-spending-categories-uk/

6   Amadeo, K. (2017). *Consumer Spending Statistics and Current Trends.* The Balance. https://www.thebalance.com/consumer-spending-trends-and-current-statistics-3305916

7   *Growing Consumption.* The European Commission. https://ec.europa.eu/knowledge4policy/foresight/topic/growing-consumerism_en

8   Sheridan, K. (2017). Richer countries are more anxious than poorer countries. *Stat News.* https://www.statnews.com/2017/03/15/anxiety-rich-country-poor-country/

disorders affect 40 million adults (18.1% of the population) every year.[9] To highlight the extent of this issue in a country that prides itself on 'living the American dream', 50 million years of healthy life expectancy, 12 million days of productivity and $1 trillion of economic output is lost *every year* due to common mental disorders.[10] This was before COVID-19 put the icing on the anxiety cake.

In the Western world, it appears that a person can be so fulfilled on the outside and so blatantly 'living their best life' for the rest of us to see that they might not even realise their comfort zones are slowly eroding their mental health. Month by month, day by day, our spirits can be ground away on a cellular level until we wake up one morning with that strange mental despair and wonder where the 'old' version of ourselves has gone. We had the dreams, goals and challenges we wanted to complete, but, all of a sudden, we realise "I should" has replaced "I will", and "I can" has become overruled by "I might".

I know this because I was one of these people.

Outwardly, I had it all. A young family, a successful career that took me to glamorous locations such as the US, the Middle East and, ahem, Basingstoke. I had a kitchen with granite worktops, the full satellite TV package, a sports car on the driveway, and a partying habit that had been kept firmly in the 'weekend warrior' camp without spilling into *Requiem for a Dream* territory. Life was good.

Wasn't it?

In many ways, it was. I had a pocketful of money, a shedload of debt and a head full of dreams. I had things I wanted to accomplish, goals I wanted to smash, journeys to travel and challenges to conquer. But, over time, my comfort zone stopped being somewhere safe to retreat for rest and recovery. It became an all-consuming, suffocating, enveloping monster from which I could not escape.

---

9   *Facts and Statistics.* Anxiety and Depression Association of America. https://adaa.org/about-adaa/press-room/facts-statistics

10 Chisholm, D. et al. (2016). 'Scaling-up treatment of depression and anxiety: a global return on investment analysis'. *The Lancet.* https://www.thelancet.com/journals/lanpsy/article/PIIS2215-0366(16)30024-4/fulltext#seccestitle190

I was aware then, and remind myself now, that people in other parts of the world would pray to have these materialistic problems. In fact, I was so aware of this that I had planned to go to North Africa and help the very people who were *truly* facing hardship. And I wasn't going to support them in the way a celebrity cries crocodile tears during a charity appeal before being whisked away in a 4x4 truck to a luxury hotel. I wanted to get my hands dirty, embed myself and get shit done.

It had always been a goal of mine to give something back. I wanted to do some good in the world and, simultaneously, spark a blaze of motivation to sort my life out – to give myself a slap around the face with an anti-mosquito net and realise how bloody lucky I was.

But then the work hours got longer, and the restaurants became finer. The clothes got tighter, and the early mornings got tougher. Somewhere, over time, my motivation to challenge myself and help other people went like this:

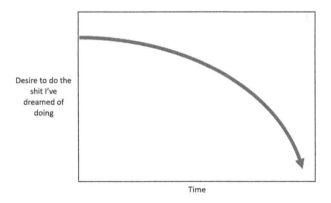

It wasn't that my get-up-and-go suddenly got up and went. I want to help others now even more so than I did back then. But that desire, that hunger to do something difficult and different and challenging and strange changed from a burning furnace to a flicker no greater than the flame of the cigarette lighter I was using while huddled in the doorway of a London nightclub at 1 am, with my suit jacket pulled up over my head to protect me from the wind and rain, like some demented, over-comforted Phantom of the Opera.

I never had a problem with self-motivation, dreaming or desire. I was once that brat with a five-year plan to test myself and explore the world while tackling every adventure I could face. My comfort zone was something to smash out of and leave broken in my wake as I bounded from one impossible challenge to the next. For a while, it worked.

Before the age of 30, I had scuba-dived on four continents, ridden camels through mountain ranges, leaped from the world's highest bungee jump, jumped from a plane, cage-dived with great white sharks, run a marathon, been stranded in the Nevada desert and explored over 40 countries. And what's more, I hadn't undertaken these activities through a bank-of-mum-and-dad glorified family excursion. I saved, planned, sweated and crawled to make these things happen. The only way I could accomplish these feats was to take the *difficult* option. The easy thing would have been to stay in my bubble with the same friends, same routines, same weekends, same holidays and same stories.

But – somewhere, somehow – it all changed. *After* the age of 30, I suffered a mental breakdown, was chased out of a country, was almost fired from work, had a gun held to my head by a drug dealer, locked my naked self out a hotel room while at a work conference, missed a lot of flights, suffered numerous blackouts and was almost fired from another job – all while deluding myself that I was having a bloody good time, living the dream and challenging myself more than ever before.

What happened? How did my comfort zone transform from something to be escaped into a vortex from which there was *no* escape and that was clearly trying to harm me?

This was the question that spun around and around inside my head like a whirlpool, late one night in a (s)wanky London hotel. As I questioned my past, my future, my actions and my decisions, it felt like my goals and dreams were sucked away into a black hole. Without warning, a bolt of inspiration hit me unexpectedly. I thought of my young baby, my house, my sports car and my recent promotion at work – and I knew with certainty what I had to do.

It was time to kill myself.

MR MOTIVATOR

Therefore, I may not be winning any awards for 'Most Likely To Write a Motivational Book'. That's fine. I didn't write this book to coach, motivate or inspire. There are plenty of people out there with much better teeth and more Botox than me who are amazing at firing people up to conquer the world.

But what happens *after* people have been motivated, energised and galvanised? We attend the seminars, read the books and watch the YouTube videos, and it feels like a rocket of exhilaration has been fired up our arses.

We tell ourselves, "*This is it!* We are going to go and do it!"

We make the plans, write the journals, create the vision boards and tell our friends about all the amazing dreams we are going to make happen almost *immediately*. But, in truth, the phrases we use with our loved ones tend to follow a familiar pattern:

"I'm *so* inspired! It's time to make the most of my life, and I don't want to waste a second! I'm going to book that trip/skydive/adventure/ challenge I've had my eye on for so long. Let's do this!"

Then…

"I am feeling energised and ready to go! I can't believe how much excitement I have for this trip/skydive/adventure/challenge; it is going to be amazing! I'll just get this project out of the way and then it's going to *happen*."

Followed by…

"I can't wait to do this trip/skydive/adventure/challenge. When I book it next year, it will be the best decision I ever made."

And…

"I've always wanted to do a trip/skydive/adventure/challenge, just as soon as COVID-19/the economy/my fitness/my marriage/ the European Union/the value of my house/little Albert's school grades/climate change is back on track, then I'll start looking into it."

Until you reach…

"You know what kind of people go on that trip/skydive/adventure/ challenge? Arseholes, that's who. Boring, selfish arseholes. They would be much better off putting that money into a mortgage. I looked into that trip/skydive/adventure/challenge once, and it was a total waste of time."

Then, before you know it, your comfort zone has once again pulled you back in and trapped you in a bubble of regret. And the real beauty of it? You didn't even notice you were doing it to yourself.

I had versions of these conversations so many times over the years. So often, I would get inspired to undertake some great challenge or adventure. I would spend sleepless nights imagining myself doing the activity and feeling the sensations, my ears tingling with the imaginary awe and praise from my friends. I would waste hours at work finding out about a hot, new activity – skydiving or kitesurfing, for example – reading articles, watching videos and buying books on Amazon that were destined to become a pile on my bedside table like a tombstone of a life I wished for.

However, when it came to the moment at which I had to take the leap and commit to the activity, and when I had to make that tiny-but-monumental shift from *thinking* to *doing*, I always stepped back from the edge. Over the years, I developed a real talent for dodging these potentially life-enhancing and life-changing events. Once again, my devious comfort zone was ready to whisper some poison into my ear to divert me from my chosen path:

- "You don't have the money" – Adventures, activities and challenges weren't free or cheap. Sure, there were things in my life I needed to prioritise my spending on, rather than heading off on crazy new challenges. Things such as mortgages, food, nappies, asthma medication and stuff like that. But I lost count of the nights I spent saying, "I'd love to try that challenge... but I can't afford it," while kicking off my hideous Gucci trainers, switching on Netflix and shoving my mouth full of takeaway pizza.

- "You're too busy" – Sooooooo busy. What with work, family, sleeping, eating, drinking, partying, Netflix watching, spending hours browsing online trying to find some even more hideous Gucci trainers to spend money on, that night out I couldn't miss, and the resulting hangover that sure as hell couldn't miss me. How could I possibly free up some of my calendar to waste time on some shitty, unique, exhilarating, breathtaking adventure? But if I ever did manage to find a small window of opportunity, I'd make sure I spent it productively: thinking about what I wanted to do, maybe even watching a video of other people doing it, and wishing I could be one of those people. If only I hadn't been so busy.

- "You don't have the skills" – Bear Grylls showed me feats of adventure I couldn't possibly begin to fathom. Watching Alex Honnold scale El Capitan's 900-metre vertical rock face at Yosemite National Park without ropes, I was so shocked that I almost forgot to renew my Netflix subscription. When Dame Ellen MacArthur became the first woman to sail around the world solo, I nearly dropped my beer and choked on my pizza. These people inspired me to go on adventures and find new challenges. But then I realised that, surely, *I* couldn't do these things? These people were experts. They had strengths that I didn't. They had knowledge and expertise. They had skills. They had never been beginners once. Evidently, they had never failed at anything. I would just have to accept that these celebrities had the right stuff. And as my comfort zone reminded me, I did not.

- "You are going to look stupid" – If I did manage to partake in my chosen breathtaking challenge, I would look so unfathomably foolish I would never live it down. Attempt an obstacle-course race? My comfort zone conjured up an image of a mud-caked Bambi on ice. Abseiling? An image of a greased, cooked duck hanging in a shop window in Chinatown would spring to mind. Downhill mountain-biking? Everyone loves a picture of a man impaled through the arse by a tree branch, like an extra from

Game of Thrones. Even if I did want to try something new, there was no way *I* was going to look stupid. Sure, I'd walked around a wedding in my underwear and there was that drunken 'accident' with the vacuum cleaner that meant I'd needed to be fitted with a catheter for six weeks. But try something new? Not me; I had a reputation to uphold.

No matter which devious path my comfort zone took – whether it moved silently and stealthily, like an emotional special forces platoon, or carpet-bombed my dreams as if I were an oil-rich state – the outcome would always be the same. I'd discover, dream and get excited… and then convince myself it just couldn't be done. Or to be precise, it absolutely *could* be achieved, just not by someone like me.

But what had changed? How did I go from being a dreamer and a someday-sayer to grabbing my life and taking action? I was on a runaway train to an existence of total, mindless, beige, life-sapping comfort, staring wistfully out of the window at the dreams and goals I once had, and telling myself it was OK. It was normal to not do the things I wanted to do. It was fine to dream but not achieve. It was good that other people did these things, but not me.

Then I realised it wasn't OK. I decided I wanted to punch my comfort zone in the dick

There wasn't one motivational speaker who invigorated me more than the rest. I didn't watch my 5,001st inspirational video on YouTube and reach a tipping point suddenly where my barrel of determination runneth over. I realised that it wasn't about gaining motivation and inspiration from the outside world at all. I always had the dreams, hopes and goals inside me, sloshing around like perfectly good petrol in a wrecked and rusty car; I just needed the spark to ignite it. And that catalyst wasn't motivation at all.

It was time.

Or, to be precise, the lack of it.

FATHERLY ADVICE

Growing up, my dad was a fountain of insight and inspiration.

He taught me that debt collectors can't enter your house and seize your possessions if you hide behind the sofa and send your nine-year-old son to answer the door. I observed the subtle art of smoking 20 Silk Cuts and drinking three bottles of wine every night, and then bouncing out of bed the next day to listen to *The Archers* on BBC Radio 4. I learned when it's your son's 18th birthday, it's frowned upon to joke, "I haven't got you a present, but, FYI, I'm fucking your mum's best friend."

But, despite all this, I love him dearly and could never ask for a different – or better – father. Plus, he enlightened me with the most important lesson I have ever received in my life: time is short.

Rather selfishly, in my opinion, he taught me that lesson by dying.

I woke on 8th September 2016, fumbled with the alarm clock as if it had caused me some injustice during the night, rose and frowned at my reflection. *Just like any other day.* On the train to work, I scrolled through Instagram, looking at adventures, liking the posts of other people who had achieved some amazing feat, and telling myself I'd quite like a challenge – someday. *Just like any other day.* I staggered into my office like a zombie, with a familiar aching inside my head: that nagging, relentless voice interrogating me, asking, "Is this really *it*? Is this how it's supposed to be?" *Just like any other day.*

I slouched at my desk, with my chin in the palm of my hand, looking at my computer monitor with glazed eyes, and moaning to a colleague about a corrupted spreadsheet that had literally ruined my life. *Just like any other day.*

Then the phone rang, and I realised this was not just any other day: this was the day my life changed forever.

We always imagine getting the phone call. We wonder morbidly how we will react. Will we become panicked and tearful? Or do we develop the calm tunnel vision and laser focus of a sniper observing death with an emotionless, almost psychopathic coolness? No matter how we think we are going to feel, two things are always true: it never happens the way we think it will, and – like so many things – we consider it to be something we see happening to other people and on TV, but never assume it will be part of our lives.

I don't remember much of the frantic phone calls between the hospital, family members and me, only the odd word: 'ambulance', 'intensive care', and, comically, 'very poorly'. I almost smiled, as I'd used the very same symptoms to describe a killer hangover the week before.

As I went from annoyance that my day had been interrupted to concern, to shock and then to fear, it would make a better story if I said I dropped to the floor and wailed. It would make me sound like a stronger person if I told you I handled things with calm precision. But the honest truth is that my responses started with, "Shit" and then turned to, "Fuck".

After five hours and 300 frantically driven miles, in which the only distraction to pull me out of my thoughts were the flashes from speed cameras as I sped past, I was standing in an intensive care unit. Looking down at my unconscious father, I wondered if, when he was enjoying his first coffee and cigarette earlier in the day, he had any idea that he may never see another sunrise, enjoy another glass of wine or set eyes on his grandchildren again. If he had known, would he have done anything about it? Would he have stopped at nothing to ensure this day was not his last? Would he have fought, kicking and screaming with every last ounce of strength, and refusing to accept the odds were stacked against him? Or would he have smiled and shrugged his shoulders, confident that he had no regrets and wrapped in the comfort of knowing that he had done everything he ever wanted to do?

After being ushered quietly into a room no bigger than a storage closet, I was instructed to sit on a cheap plastic chair, with rust creeping up the uneven metallic legs from a decade of being soaked in anti-bacterial cleaning agents. Two doctors, who were not much older than me, began the intricate balancing act of explaining what was happening to my father and pretending they had all the time in the world to talk to me while taking hidden glances at their watches, fully aware that, as always, they had too many patients to see and not enough hours in the day. They described what had happened to my dad just a few hours earlier, and detailed how they had kept him alive long enough to ensure I would arrive in time to say goodbye.

"How did you manage that?" I asked, unaware that doctors have the power to control – to some extent at least – when a seriously ill patient would shuffle off their mortal coil.

"Adrenaline," the medic replied. "We kept him alive with adrenaline."

It barely registered in my shocked and numb brain at the time, but I pondered this question later that night when I was sitting on my father's sofa, still wearing my dishevelled work suit, as I ploughed through his wine collection like a man on a mission.

Although my dad was surrounded by some of the best medical technology and drugs the modern world had to offer, and even though he had teams of highly skilled and educated practitioners working on his failing body, there was only one thing keeping him alive: the naturally occurring chemical of adrenaline.

I had chuckled to myself as I sat in the gloomy darkness of his lounge, with the only light seemingly being emitted from the walls stained nicotine-yellow. The irony was not lost on me that my dad had spent so many years avoiding any kind of adrenaline, yet it was that very substance that had kept him alive long enough for me to say goodbye.

The complex array of monitors beeped an urgent symphony of despair as the adrenaline being administered into my father's veins was withdrawn. My world closed in on me as I watched his breathing become slower and shallower. Then – in that early Thursday evening when the rest of the world was eating, watching TV, thinking, dreaming, arguing or loving – I watched my dad die. I bent down and awkwardly placed a kiss upon his forehead (it's a bit weird for a 35-year-old man to kiss his father, after all), told him I loved him and said goodbye.

In the stunned hours that followed, there were those broken, repetitive discussions when you have to call family members and have the same conversation half a dozen times: "No, I'm not joking," "Yes, he is really dead," and "No, he wasn't having sex when it happened."

It was one of those confusing, fragmented sections of life when time seems to stand still but simultaneously runs so fast that everything around you seems blurred, in which one thought kept rising to the surface of my mind: I thought about my dad's life, about all the marriages, children, disputes, arguments, conflicts, stubbornness, deceit, prisons of lies and walls of silence.

Now, none of it mattered. People in his life had spent weeks, months and even years of their existence worrying, stressing, pleading and wringing their hands, all using up so much of their time and energy. And now he was gone. His time was over, and so much hope, so much potential, had been turned to dust.

I had just received the world's most effective training course in time being short and life being precious, and I hadn't needed to pay a penny. It had, however, cost me my dad.

Now, in the Disney version of this story, the moment I made that sudden, stolen goodbye to my father would have set the stage for my rebirth. I would have risen like a phoenix from his ashes, determined to make the very best of my life and savour every opportunity it presented me. *After all,* I told myself, *you only live once* [YOLO].

The reality, however, is somewhat, well, different.

I took the often-quoted YOLO mantra and I tore the arse out of it. I drank and partied like there was no tomorrow. I consumed liquid and chemical breakfasts that would make a rock star turn away in disgust. I gave up trying at work and kicked the 'professional' caricature version of myself into the gutter, no longer hiding my disgust for spreadsheets, profit forecasts and making money for a boss who I had never even met. I was thrown out of bars, escorted off flights, banned from hotels, hauled in front of human resources (HR), and subjected to endless messages and emails from friends and family members voicing their concern.

I had created a new comfort zone for myself and I absolutely loved it. I was swaddled in the cosy embrace of alcohol, junk food, late nights and lazy days in front of the TV. Nothing says 'high achiever' like watching Netflix in your underwear with a beer in your hand. At 10am. On a weekday.

It wasn't all downhill, of course. Every now and then, usually when I was being subjected to one of those hangovers that felt like a hand had been rummaging in a dustbin before being shoved down your throat and squeezing your internal organs as tightly as possible, I had a vague feeling that something needed to change. I still wanted to do all the things I'd dreamed of. I supposed it would be nice to not drink myself into an early gave. Every now and then, I even toyed with the idea of making my kids proud of me. Once or twice, the urge was so strong that I even bought a self-help book or watched a motivational video on YouTube. The outcome was always the same: the book would be added to the pile, and YouTube would be switched to a website that was more, ahem, exotic. My comfort zone would always win.

But one day, in February 2017, something did change. It wasn't a New Year's resolution, and I hadn't yet considered anything as ridiculous as quitting alcohol, but something sparked in my tired, stressed, defeated brain. Sitting in front of another computer monitor at another desk in another office, I was idly browsing a plethora of different adventures to try. My eyes fell upon the legendary Marathon des Sables (meaning the Marathon of the Sands), which is an iconic 200-mile, self-supported, ultramarathon across the Sahara Desert. It wasn't the race distance that caught my attention, nor the searing heat, extreme conditions, rationed water or poisonous creatures. It was the title: 'The World's Toughest Footrace'. There was something so intimidating about it, so imposing and so impossibly beautiful yet absolutely terrifying.

As if in a trance, I pulled out my credit card. At this sudden, unexpected action, my comfort zone jolted awake from its slumber. I could almost picture this frowning, angry, grey creature running around inside me, like a submarine captain in a war movie when the bridge is bathed in flashing, red lights as he realises his boat is about to receive the good news from an enemy torpedo at any moment.

As I began completing the online application, my comfort zone took emergency action:

<Enter name and address>

You're not fit enough. This is the world's toughest footrace, for God's sake! The only thing you can run up is a bar bill!

<Please provide credit card details>

You can't afford it! Remember that night out last month that cost the same as a mortgage payment? You won't be able to pay your bills if you do this!

<Please sign electronic waiver that you accept the risk of death>

Everyone will laugh at you! What if you fail? What if you get hurt? If you die, they will shout, "We told you so," at your graveside!

But for once and for some reason unknown to me at the time, I closed my ears to the desperate, pleading wails of my comfort zone. I turned away from the well-trodden, heavily soaked route of comfort, safety and ease. I chose another way. My path took me in a different direction:

- Running through the Sahara Desert and finishing the world's toughest footrace
- Breaking a Guinness World Record
- Becoming an Ironman
- Completing ten marathons
- Winning a 70-mile all-night ultramarathon
- Leaping from the world's highest bungee jump
- Diving with great white sharks
- Walking on fire
- Completing the UK's first 'lockdown ultramarathon', running 46 miles around my tiny garden.

But what made me do this? After being a prisoner to my comfort zone for so long, what enabled me to break free? I'm not an athlete;

I've never been in the military; my upbringing was in no way focused on adventure, the outdoors or trying to challenge myself; and I have no unique or especially defining characteristics whatsoever. I'm just an ordinary person who decided to escape my comfort zone and do extraordinary things. And if I could do it, then so can you.

And this, my friends, is how…

THREE

KNOW YOUR ENEMY

"The comfort zone is a psychological state in which one feels familiar, safe, at ease, and secure. You never change your life until you step out of your comfort zone; change begins at the end of your comfort zone."

Roy T. Bennett (no relation)

When did the comfort zone start to get such a hard time?

For thousands of years, humanity has fought, learned, tried, failed and struggled to increase the level of comfort in our lives by just a small percentage. Even today, over a billion people are trapped in the extreme opposite of what we would describe as a 'comfortable standard of living'. Yet, in modern Western civilisation, our comfort zones have become something unpleasant. They have evolved to be something that is tolerated with a roll of the eyes and a knowing look of begrudging acceptance. It's like we have spent a millennia striving to create the perfect conditions to welcome this high standard of prosperity into our lives, but then the comfort zone shows up at its own party, only to be told it's no longer welcome.

We are bombarded with material telling us to push ourselves

harder, act faster and think on a higher level of consciousness. But is relaxing in the warm cuddle of comfort *such* a bad thing? It's not as if humanity had it easy, and things aren't exactly plain sailing right now. What's wrong with kicking back, getting comfortable, opening a cold one and saying cheers to the fact we've somehow made it this far (at the time of writing) through a global pandemic.

So, turn the heating up, tell Amazon to deliver that thing to your door and make yourself another flat white, because things are about to get comfortable…

GETTING COMFORTABLE

The concept of the comfort zone has been around for a while. While the actual phrase did not enter the English language until the late 1990s (coincidentally, around the same time as the two behemoths of comfort – the internet and the mobile phone – started to make a noticeable impact on human behaviour), the theory of 'living in comfort' became a thing just after the start of the 20th century. Or, in other words, when life started to become more comfortable.

The comfort zone started, somewhat unexpectedly, with a dancing mouse. In 1908, two psychologists, Robert Yerkes and John Dodson, identified a relationship between arousal and performance. The aptly named Yerkes-Dodson law proves that a creature's performance level increases when they experience physiological or mental arousal – but only up to a point.[11] When the levels of arousal become too high, and excitement turns into pressure and then into stress, performance starts to plummet like a kid falling from a dodgy zipline.

So, in other words, let's say I don't like doing press-ups (and in the period from 1982–2017 this was definitely the case). If I had sprawled out begrudgingly on the floor, I'd probably give you five or six at best. Then my comfort zone would start to hammer on the wall and tell

---

11   Yerkes, R.M. & Dodson, J.D. (1908). The relation of strength of stimulus to rapidity of habit-formation. *Journal of Comparative Neurology and Psychology*. 18(5): 459–482.

me give it a rest. If you happened to walk by and shout some words of encouragement, I'd do my best to squeeze out a couple more. When you started to do your best impression of Gunnery Sergeant Hartman from *Full Metal Jacket* and scream in my face, I'd most likely muster up another press-up before my comfort zone threw up its hands in despair, pulled the plug and told you to go fuck yourself. Then if you pulled a gun on me and told me you'd shoot me if I didn't do five more, I might manage it – but you would most certainly be off my Christmas-card list.

The point that the Yerkes-Dodson law makes is that different tasks need a different level of arousal for performance. So, going from zero to smashing through a glass ceiling of comfort isn't always the best idea.

While the research of Yerkes and Dodson was groundbreaking in its time, there was a slight issue. Their psychological experiments had not been conducted with humans, but with dancing mice. Imagine my disappointment when I discovered that a dancing mouse is a breed of mouse, not a mouse that dances.

It's unsurprising that the first indications of the comfort zone were shown in animals rather than humans. After all, humanity had a lot on its plate around the same time: World War I for starters, followed by the Spanish flu pandemic (sounds familiar), the birth of Hitler, World War II and the subsequent Cold War served up a tasty dessert of the constant threat of nuclear annihilation. For decades, humans were more preoccupied with staying alive and praying the world didn't obliterate itself rather than debating whether they should go to CrossFit or order something from Uber Eats instead.

Although the comfort zone was formally introduced to human society relatively recently, its origins lie in the deeper, darker, animalistic mists of human evolution. Since the rise of Homo sapiens, we have sought safety and comfort. In fact, we would not be here today unless our distant ancestors had made the instinctive decision to seek out comfort. Sure, a cave was handy, and discovering fire certainly made life easier, but we aren't exactly talking about a suite at the Ritz. However, for humanity to survive, evolve, adapt and thrive, we knew instinctively to seek a certain level of comfort.

In 1943, American psychologist Abraham Maslow published his iconic paper, 'A Theory of Human Motivation'.[12] This theory comprises a five-tier model of human needs, which is generally known as Maslow's hierarchy of needs. Maslow believes that humans not only need these external influences to survive, but they are also the key to our development as a species. These needs cover areas of our lives such as *self-actualisation* (reaching our own potential), *esteem* (feeling self-worth and accomplishment), *love* and belonging (friends and intimate relationships). However, the sting in the tail is that *none* of these can be met unless our basic needs are taken care of. Physiological needs such as food, water, warmth and rest form the bedrock and foundations of this model. Food, water, warmth and rest also have a shorter definition. One word, two syllables: *comfort*.

Around 10,000 years ago, humans needed literally to create a physical 'zone of comfort' around themselves, because if they didn't, then they would die. If we absolutely *have* to do something day after day, year after year, and generation after generation, it becomes ingrained in our psyche and the essence of who we are. This is still true today. Are you worried about how to overcome doubts around self-fulfilment? Then set your house on fire.* It will make you realise that you have some more basic needs to focus on, and, suddenly, that nagging urge to discover your true inner self will take a back seat for a few days.

Our comfort zones are not something that abruptly jumped out on us one day; looking back through history, we sought out these comfort zones and actively brought them into our lives. We had no choice! Whether it was a cave, a mud hut, a treehouse or a tent surrounded by a ring of thorns, we knew instinctively that creating a zone of comfort around ourselves was essential. We were just too preoccupied with hunting, breeding, learning, inventing and evolving

---

12   Maslow, A.H. (1943). 'A theory of human motivation'. *Psychological Review*. 50(4), 370-396

*   Do not set your house on fire.

to think anything of it. Our comfort zones became an essential part of our lives, hiding in plain sight.

After hiding away from us for so long, the comfort zone started to make an appearance in the early 1990s. True to the era, if your comfort zone had an appearance, it would be wearing a shell suit and have a Sony Discman clipped to its neon-green bumbag. Why did the comfort zone choose to arrive and shout, *"Most excellent, dudes!"* (*a la Bill and Ted's Excellent Adventure*) at this particular point in human history, you ask? It comes down to two small-but-very-impactful words: *money* and *time*.

They say money makes the world go round. And from the mid-1980s onwards, we were spinning right round. The year 1992 had seen Black Wednesday when the collapse in the pound sterling forced Britain to withdraw from the European Exchange Rate Mechanism (ERM). Times were dull for a while, but, like the day Hugh Hefner discovered Viagra, what goes down will soon shoot up – like a rocket.

Data from the UK Office for National Statistics[13] shows us that, from 1995, disposable household income went on a one-way ticket to outer space. For those of us who aren't economists, 'disposable income' means having more money to spend on shit such as trainers, holidays, TVs, sofas, booze and drugs. Gross domestic product (GDP) followed a similar pattern during that time, while unemployment fell throughout the decade. Tony Blair flashed his dazzling grin from the steps of 10 Downing Street, and Cool Britannia ruled the waves: life was good.

This wasn't just a party that the UK was invited to. Patterns were similar in the US. The US Census Bureau identified that real median household income in the US was $52,942 in 1994 and rose rapidly to $60,062 by 1999.[14] Now this might not sound like a lot, but imagine sitting in your home in 1999 and realising you had an extra $7,000 to spend on trainers, CDs, big-screen TVs and drugs compared to what you did five years earlier. You'd most likely be tempted to go out and party like you've been warned the bars and restaurants will be shut down again.

---

13   https://www.ons.gov.uk/peoplepopulationandcommunity/
     personalandhouseholdfinances/incomeandwealth/bulletins/
     householddisposableincomeandinequality/financialyearending2016
14   https://fred.stlouisfed.org/series/MEHOINUSA672N

So, people around the Western world were getting more money than they ever had before, and they were using it to make themselves more 'comfortable'. How many times have you heard a smugly smiling friend, relative or colleague utter the words, "We're comfortable"? And, if they were being a typically polite and repressed Brit, this phrase would actually mean they were wiping their arses with £20 notes and swimming in a pool full of cash. This is by no means a rant about society, what else would you expect people to do? Not so long ago, life was bloody hard. War was still a dark, not-that-distant memory in people's conscience. Grandparents would talk of rationing, and the West and Russia were packing away their nuclear weapons like a child who has lost a game of football and storms off home, taking the ball with him.

But – in a decade when money was plentiful, credit was cheap and greed was still good – can you really blame people for making their comfort zones as big, cushioned and plentiful as possible? I certainly can't. But as the 1990s turned to the 2000s – and the millennium bug turned out to be the biggest load of hot air in history until someone said, "They'll never vote to leave the European Union" – another factor came into play. Ironically, this was also the one thing money couldn't buy: *time*.

Since 2000, the way we spend our time has changed drastically. According to Professor Jesse Ausubel from Rockefeller University, people have been overdosing on 'Netflix and chill' like never before. According to Ausubel, a British worker in 1960 spent 11.72% of his or her life working.[15] By 2010, that number had dropped to 8.77%, suggesting that a typical Briton had more time to spend on other things. The US, France, Germany and, to a lesser extent, Japan saw similar reductions.[16]

Who do we have to thank for this excessive amount of time we

---

15   Ausbel, JH (1995). 'Working Less and Living Longer: Long-Term Trends in Working Time and Time Budget'. *Technological Forecasting and Social Change* 50: 113–13

16   *Doing Business, trading across borders* (n.d.). Human Progress. https://www.humanprogress.org/dataset/doing-business-trading-across-borders-documents-to-export/

have on our hands? Well, you should be tipping your cap to Messrs Gates, Berners-Lee, Jobs and their buddies in Silicon Valley, because technology holds the key to our lives of leisure.

Technology has been making our lives easier since the industrial revolution – unless your great-grandparent lost their job to a shiny, new mechanical loom in a 19th-century cotton mill – but, on the bright side, at least they had a lot more time on their hands. However, it was the dawn of the internet that really turned our comfort dials up to 11. Although the World Wide Web became publicly available on 6th August 1991, it did not start to impact people's working, shopping and pornography habits significantly until the early 2000s. Before then, we still had to visit shops, libraries and reach for the top shelf in newsagents to get what we needed. Manually producing and obtaining all this information took up valuable time. This was fine, it was a 'normal' level of comfort, and our comfort zones were kept in check because this was just how life was supposed to be.

But in 2007, on a crisp January day in San Francisco, Steve Jobs finished his Macworld keynote speech with, "Just one more thing…" and fished a rectangular object from his project. With a flourish, he introduced a "breakthrough internet communications device" to rapturous applause. This adulation drowned out another noise – the sound of tens of millions of comfort zones breathing out contented sighs of relief, putting on some comfy pants and ordering a takeaway – because life was about to get a *whole* lot easier for people.

The comfort revolution did not occur overnight, but the change was rapid, and when measured over the course of human evolution, it happened in the blink of an eye. Suddenly, the internet was in everyone's pocket, and – boosted by iOS and Android apps – people literally had a world of information and possibilities in the palm of their hands. Mobile internet traffic exploded, growing from 14 billion bytes a month at the start of 2008 to almost 10 *trillion* bytes per month at the start of 2017.[17]

---

17 https://www.vox.com/2017/6/26/15821652/iphone-apple-10-year-anniversary-launch-mobile-stats-smart-phone-steve-jobs

The if the internet fed our comfort zones by opening our eyes to all the information in the world, then the iPhone told it to lie back and open up like a foie gras goose on force-feeding day. Before Apple calls the lawyers, however, I must say iPhones were not the only culprit, but they were the canary in the mineshaft for a world that was adapting to and embracing technology like never before.

Before we knew it, modern technology was saving us time we didn't even know we had. Today, technology saves the average person two weeks each year that would otherwise be spent on boring, time-consuming tasks such as shopping and banking. A 2018 UK study shows technology was saving us an average of 21 minutes per week on banking, satnavs save us 21 minutes per week sitting in traffic jams, online food shopping frees up another 23 minutes per week, and self-service checkouts, online travel timetables and contactless payments each save us more than 10 minutes per week each.[18]

Quite simply, technology gives us more time than ever before because it does more for us, brings more things to our door, lets us make faster decisions and helps us do things with far less effort. I realised this when I discovered that my four-year-old could create and order his own pizza to be delivered to our door. When I was four years old, back in the 1980s, a good day for me would involve sticking Lego up my bum, not organising a meal for my family.

So, thanks to the dual forces of time and money, life is wonderful. We earn more, work less and have more leisure time. Sounds great, right?

Wrong.

---

18   https://www.independent.co.uk/life-style/technology-time-saving-self-service-shopping-online-banking-tasks-study-a8668281.html

"COME WITH ME IF YOU WANT TO LIVE"[19]

Our comfort zones were our best friend for thousands of years. Creating a zone of comfort allowed us to reproduce and evolve, but, like all things, our comfort zones were not perfect. As we've just seen, our cosy companion became corrupted by those two irresistible forces of money and time.

It is probably worth pointing out that I am not an enemy of time nor money. In fact, I am a huge supporter of both these concepts, despite seemingly possessing very little of each. I am not on some kind of revolutionary crusade against the forces of capitalism and technology, like some hemp-sandal wearing, soap-dodging version of Sarah Connor from the *Terminator* movie franchise. What I do believe, however, is that an abundance of time and money in our lives has been sucked up by our comfort zones like a storm gaining energy from the sea, and now we are threatened by a Category 5 hurricane of comfort that is threatening to kill us.

OK, maybe that is slightly melodramatic. And the truth is that, thanks to an abundance of time of money, our lives are likely to be longer than ever. Nonetheless, unless we can escape our comfort zones, we risk dying decades before we get buried in the ground.

It's not as crazy as it sounds. The academics at the World Health Organization (WHO) – an institute not known for its love of jokes – state: "Insufficient physical activity is one of the leading risk factors for death worldwide... [and] is a key risk factor for noncommunicable diseases (NCDs) such as cardiovascular diseases, cancer and diabetes."[20]

According to the WHO, people living in high-income countries are deemed most at risk, where 26% of men and 35% of women are insufficiently physically active. One of the key factors in this lack of activity is 'inaction during leisure time and sedentary behaviour on

19   Cameron, J. (director) (1984). *The Terminator.* [Motion picture]
20   Physical Activity. (2018). World Health Organisation. https://www.who.int/news-room/fact-sheets/detail/physical-activity

the job and at home.' In non-medical speak, this translates as 'too much time sitting on our arses in our big, fat comfort zones'. So, the evidence indicates that our comfort zones are damaging us physically. Strike one.

What about our minds? Surely, with all of this time on our hands and with technology at our fingertips, even if our bodies are a bloated and flailing disaster, like the Hindenburg at a fireworks display, shouldn't our brains be sharper and more stimulated than ever?

Unfortunately not.

Our brains *love* comfort. And not in the way a CrossFit junkie loves it when someone asks them, "What do you do for fun?" Our minds love comfort in the way an addict loves heroin. And to quote the judge when he handed me the restraining order, "There is such a thing as the wrong kind of love."

We have always wanted to be in a safe environment with the minimal amount of risk and stress. Once again, this goes back to the good old prehistoric days when we evolved to prefer a life in a cave with our feet up, looking at the drawings on the wall and munching on some barbecued mammoth, rather than being chased by a sabre-toothed tiger. This still applies today, and when we are offered a more comfortable, safer option, we are always naturally inclined to take it. Who wouldn't? We encourage each other to 'play it safe' and 'take it easy' because that is what we instinctively want for ourselves.

We also seek out comfort because it conserves energy. As our brain needs so much energy to function and to process the 60,000–80,000 thoughts running through it every day, it is always searching for any habit, shortcut or neural pathway it can possibly find to make life easier. It's like the mother of the bride running around on the morning of her daughter's wedding. Do you *really* want to approach and tell her that the wedding cake is pink and one of the bridesmaids has overdosed in the toilet? Or do you want to take a more comfortable approach and not overload her with any additional drama?

The eternal search for comfort has kept our brains (and the rest of our bodies) alive for so long, but comfort is now starting to kill it.

Like our muscles, our brains need stimulation to grow. If we don't challenge our minds, and provide fear, nervousness, excitement, trials, learning and love, then the information stops flowing, like water trying to traverse a blocked river. This is why we sometimes wake up in a box, to travel to work in a box, to spend eight hours sitting in a box, travel home in a box, watch the box while eating out of a box… And then we struggle to remember what happened that day. If we repeat this too many times, we will find ourselves lying in a box for eternity, wondering why we didn't do something different.

No matter what we do in life, if we do it again and again, day after day, our comfort zones become more and more content. A rollercoaster is thrilling the first time around, but when Richard Rodriguez sat on one for nine days to break the Guinness World Record for the longest rollercoaster marathon, his brain became so comfortable that he was able to fall asleep for hours at a time. On a similar-but-less-impressive note, when I first watched the movie *Showgirls* as a 14-year-old boy, I found it extremely, ahem, stimulating. But by the 50th viewing it was like being slapped in the face by a cold fish. In order to save you from the mental image of that particular experience, we can agree that our comfort zones are also shooting us right between the eyes mentally: strike two.

So far, our comfort zones have begun to look like an over-friendly Hollywood actor during the rise of the #MeToo movement: loved and adored for so many years, but when you start to dig a little deeper, they are actually a piece of shit.

And the bad news is that our comfort zones aren't just being inappropriate when it comes to our bodies and minds: professionally, they cause us damage as well. No matter what we say on our LinkedIn profile, the majority will naturally try to make their working life as easy as possible. We've all glanced up from a busy day surfing the internet in the office and given a colleague a nudge to point out the person who is always making life so *difficult* for themselves. There would always be the one co-worker who, if given an empty bucket and instructed to carry it around all day, would fill it full of water, just to make the task harder.

"*Why do they do it?*" we ask each other over the work WhatsApp chat group. "When will they ever learn to take it easy?"

The billionaire software magnate Bill Gates – a man not associated with kicking back and chilling out – once said, "I will always choose a lazy person to do a difficult job because a lazy person will find an easy way to do it." So if one of the richest people on the planet is OK with people staying in their comfort zones, then it's cool, right?

Absolutely right, comrade. If your sole aim in life is to help a billionaire become even richer.

In fact, our comfort zones try every trick in the book to make us commit career suicide. Like an industrial workhouse master in a Charles Dickens novel, it will use fear, ridicule, praise and psychological warfare to keep us in our place and prevent us from thinking we could take our careers any further.

In my previous profession, I spent years fighting tooth and nail to avoid any kind of change in my role that would involve doing a different task, meeting intimidating senior stakeholders, travelling to distant lands or risking failure. The truth was that I desperately *wanted* to do these things and, deep down, I knew I could do a bloody brilliant job. But every time I plucked up the courage, faced my fears and prepared to take the leap into the unknown, my comfort zone would pull me back from the precipice, whispering sweet nothings in my ear about 'work–life balance', 'jeopardising promotion prospects' or 'not being a team player'.

Low and behold, whenever I listened to that comfort zone and took the easy route, my career started to mimic the trajectory of Blockbuster Video stores at around 2007. Strike three.

Much as I hate to kick a creature when it's down (or at all, for that matter), if damaging our bodies, minds and careers wasn't bad enough, the whole *perception* of our comfort zone comes under attack in modern society. Just like in days gone by when a certain brown-coloured soft drink used to boast about its cocaine content, or when doctors told us that we really should be aiming to smoke at least 10 cigarettes per day to make our lungs stronger, a comfort zone used to be a great thing to have. Today, even being associated with such a concept is viewed with disgust.

In today's world, a comfort zone is not something to be obtained, it is to be *avoided* at all costs. A comfort zone bypasses financial status, age, ethnicity, gender, race and sexual orientation. It is one of the few things in life that does not discriminate who it inflicts dream-limiting pain upon. Let's look at an economic example.

If you are in your comfort zone and rich, then you are perceived as a fat cat, out of touch, privileged, sheltered, over-entitled and overindulged. People will look up at you in your ivory tower and sneer, while muttering that you have no idea what a day of hardship feels like. You are also probably a politician or banker, so congratulations on fucking things up so much over the past 10 years or so.

If you're residing in your comfort zone and poor, then you're regarded as a lazy waste of space with no drive and a frustrating lack of desire to do anything with your life. You're a careless stoner with no regard for the world you pollute with your pointless existence. You and I probably also frequented the same bars, so make sure you come and say hello if you see me.

But if you're rich and striving to get *out* of your comfort zone, then colleagues will say you're driven, focused and determined. You know your strengths and have no weaknesses. You've read the articles, done the courses and got the job. You're a maverick who gets results without breaking the mould. You'll get the promotion, the pay rise and the damn corner office. You're also probably a fabulous liar, but who cares about telling the truth when you love facing your fears and getting so bloody *uncomfortable*?

Escaping that comfort zone when you're poor? Then you're seen as a hustler, an entrepreneur, a haggler, a wheeler-dealer and an emperor of the gig economy. You're the kind of charismatic dreamer who's going to get all way to the top using charm alone. They'll say you'll either go to prison or be a millionaire, but you know you'll never taste cold porridge or feel another man's stubble on your back. Sleeping on a sofa, selling drugs and playing Xbox all day has just been a gap-filler – for the past eight years.

And if you can't see yourself in any of the above, then congratulations and welcome to the middle class.

The point here is that it doesn't matter *who* you are, if you are quietly content in your comfort zone, then – according to society – you are in the *wrong*. If you're happy, fairly stress free, relaxed and going through life just fine, then friends, strangers and trolls may categorise you in the same box as people who wear socks with sandals, get to the front row of a Coldplay concert, couldn't give two shits about Harry Potter, or spend their evenings playing Dungeons & Dragons. You are considered to have a personality defect, just because you like your life on the comfortable side.

*

So, we've seen that – after keeping us alive for thousands of years, nourishing our brains and being considered to be something to strive for – our comfort zones have become public enemy number one. Comfort zones are regarded as being bad for our health, wealth and social image. You can lie, cheat, pollute and steal, and it's merely frowned upon. But reclining in your comfort zone is thought by many to be committing one of life's great sins.

But why is this? Is it because there are so many people in the world who just want us to be the best version of ourselves? Or is it because getting people to escape their comfort zones is *big* business…

COMFORT IS CASH

At the time of writing this book, Google shows over 32 million internet articles on how to escape our comfort zones. Over 20,000 people in the US search the term 'escape my comfort zone' every day.

The hashtag *#comfortzone* has over a million posts on Instagram.

In which place in the world is the phrase 'How to escape my comfort zone' googled more than any other? Well, it's a deprived, barren, hostile land where nothing is easy and every day could be your last.

Otherwise known as the state of California.

That's right, it is in one of the most beautiful, sunny, intelligent, forward-thinking and richest places on the planet that more people are looking to escape their comfort zones than in anywhere else in the world. Admittedly, California has a lot more people than, say, Timbuktu, and for a lot of people in this state, life is certainly not as rosy as the tourism commercials would have you believe. But the same could be said for London, New York or the whole of Australia. While thousands of people in these places also *believe* they should be escaping their comfort zones, nowhere is it happening more than in the comfortable sunshine state.

This is where everyone seems to be taking air baths, doing extreme dieting, micro-dosing, submerging themselves in ice baths and partaking in parabiosis (this is injecting yourself with the blood of a younger person, which is good for ageing apparently, and also good for growing fangs and developing an aversion to stakeholders); in other words, doing anything and everything they can think of to prove to themselves (and, more importantly, other people) that they are escaping their comfort zone. In fact, the only way a comfort zone could make itself *less* popular on the West Coast would be to arrive in a 'Make America Great Again' cap and announce that marijuana was illegal once again.

It is also no coincidence that, in addition to being world capital of trying to escape our comfort zones, California is also the global headquarters for something a lot more *holistic*: the self-help and personal-development industry, which is worth $10 billion a year in the US alone.[21]

---

21   LaRosa, J. (2018). What's next for the $9.9 billion personal development industry. *Market Research Blog.* https://blog.marketresearch.com/whats-next-for-the-9-9-billion-personal-development-industry

Before we go any further down this seaweed-infused, joss-stick-scented path, which is lined with a million coaching DVDs (ask your parents) and powered by a thousand meditation apps, I want to clarify something: self-help is *good*! There are millions of people out there who have experienced and survived trauma, depression, anxiety, stress, self-hatred and self-harm, and who absolutely need, should get and *deserve* the best possible care and support from the most suitable professionals with the right qualifications. Maybe you are one of them, and if so, I wish you all the best with your journey and recovery. Even if it feels no one else is there for you, remember that *I am*. After all, it takes one to know one.

I have nothing but respect for anyone who is trying to live their own best life or help make someone else's better in some way. However, I do start to clench my coffee cup more tightly and do that weird bulging-eyeball thing when I see a lot of 'experts' trying to convince everyday people that being in their comfort zone is a 'problem' – and a problem the expert is happy to solve by selling a method, book, technique, app, device or formula.

Could it be that our comfort zones – faithful companions for the last 10,000 years – aren't actually that bad at all? Are they just victims of a smear campaign launched by 1,000 self-styled gurus who needed to create a problem in order to charge for the pleasure of solving it? Some things never go out of fashion: manners, for example. Or gravity, desire, humour, free speech, water, denim, and comfort?

For so many years, the comfort zone was the most popular kid in school. Everyone wanted to be around it. Then, in the early 2000s, the new self-help guru arrived from out of town (let's face it, probably from California) and convinced the whole class to hate the comfort zone. Am I wrong? Maybe, but there are over 4,000 books on Amazon talking about escaping our comfort zones that beg to differ.

Because the comfort zone has been labelled as such a negative thing, the self-development industry has evolved – like any good predator – to cater for this demand. Let's look at an example.

Say hello to Neil. Neil has an office job at a logistics company. He has two kids, pays the mortgage, goes somewhere sunny once a year, watches football and loves a good Netflix binge-watch. He's one of those people we mentioned earlier who is quite happy sitting safe and comfortable in the middle lane of life. He has no dreams of being on stage and getting the thumbs up and a shit-eating grin from Simon Cowell, he doesn't pine after a Lamborghini because they would be a nightmare to park at the supermarket, and he thinks a trip to the Maldives would be a waste of money because it will all be under water soon. His goals in life involve not being too overweight, having happy kids and hoping his wife will wear the sexy underwear to bed on Saturday night.

What a total, utter bastard.

Thankfully, Neil lives in the modern day where he is bombarded by articles, TV programmes and adverts telling him he's doing something wrong. Pretty soon, he's beginning to get stressed about it, which leads to anxiety. When he gets anxious, he starts to second-guess and doubt himself: "*Should I be doing more with my life? Am I wasting the opportunities I have been given? Does being in my comfort zone make me a bad husband, father or employee?*"

Perhaps he'll go on social media to take his mind off things, only to be faced with millions of so-called 'influencers' who are documenting the gleeful, daring escape from their comfort zones in photogenically choreographed brilliance. "Social media, that will make you feel better," said no one, ever.

But you know what *would* make Neil the Bastard feel better? A subscription to a YouTube channel perhaps, or maybe purchasing a coaching programme! Now his problems will be solved. He'll be like all the other daring go-getters who have escaped their comfort zones. With only a small investment, he'll solve a problem he never knew he had, and he'll become the person he never even wanted to be.

Selling an escape from a problematic comfort zone is just the latest example, but the history books are littered with stories of industries springing up to solve to the problems they themselves created.

The extreme ends of many major religions (including Christianity,

Islam and Judaism) consider homosexuality to be a sin, but will happily offer prayers, seminars or retreats (at a price, of course) to cure followers of what they classify as a 'disease'.

In 1999, we were bombarded with threats of the millennium bug, which would turn anything with a microchip into an idle lump of plastic once its internal computer flicked over to 01/01/2000. Funnily enough, the main pedlars of this rumour were the people who could make your technology 'millennium ready' for a small fee, of course.

A cigarette company got you hooked on the cancer sticks and now you want to kick the habit without resembling an extra from *The Walking Dead*? No problem, the same company will happily take your money for nicotine-enhanced tobacco-replacement products.

You're excited about getting your new smartphone (for the five whole minutes before you drop it and crack the screen)? But, wait, the latest model of phone has a special 'advancement' that means you need to buy some new headphones, charging cable or carry case. Don't worry because those nice people at the same company will give you one! In exchange for cold, hard cash.

When you look at examples such as these, is it so impossible to believe that the concept of it being a terrible thing to remain in your comfort zone has been created to convince people that they need to buy more personal-development products and consume more content?

I AM NOT YOUR COMFORT BLANKET

"Remember to look up at the stars and not down at your feet."

Professor Stephen Hawking

By now, your irony alarms may be going off, as if you've seen one of the anti-immigration crowd (you know the type) shouting about 'sending the foreigners home'. The very people who clean his house, sweep his streets, tidy his office, look after his kids, serve his coffee, deliver his parcels and will save his life when the inevitable heart attack hits.

This is, after all, a book about escaping your comfort zone, and I've just spent 5,000 words telling you why staying in your comfort zone isn't such a bad thing. I've also rambled on about the self-styled gurus who have created an environment to convince you to escape your comfort zone – by buying their product. Yet here you are, having purchased this book (I highly recommend the audio version as well, by the way). And if you stole it, well, hopefully, you felt like you were leaving your comfort zone in order to do so.

It played out like this for two reasons. Firstly, I *don't believe* you should always be looking to smash out of your comfort zone. Secondly, I am not portraying myself as the master, sage or shining light who will promise to solve your problems while making you extremely uncomfortable – a bit like the time a 'chiropractor' (with a home-printed qualification Blu-Tacked to the wall) told me I needed to get totally undressed to fix a problem with my ankle. He's now in prison.

Looking at reason one, as unpopular and unfashionable as it may be, a life of constantly challenging ourselves, and pushing our professional, personal and physical boundaries does us no favours. Our bodies and minds may be capable of amazing feats, but we are not robots. Looking at evolution once again, there was a reason why Mr and Mrs Caveman didn't immediately set up a franchise model to sell the fire they'd just created. They sat back in wonder and awe. Instinctively, they understood that recovery and mutual support are just as important as progress.

Stress, anxiety, burnout, midlife crisis, or 'just walked into the office one day and fucking lost their shit'. There are so many ways to describe the act of inviting more and more pressure on ourselves until we can't take any more. In the US, the demands of a stressful job cost US healthcare companies $46 billion every year. Anxiety caused by the conflict between work and family cost those same companies $24 billion per year, and crazy-long working hours costs $13 billion per year.[22] Yet these same people are still being told by society that the last thing they should be doing is seeking some mental-health shelter in their comfort zones.

We have comfortable things in life because we *need* them. Comfort blanket, comfort eating, comfortable clothes and creature comforts. We don't have this stuff because it sounds snazzy; these things exist because life throws so much crap at us that we have to seek out respite from the world.

I know, it's a confusing decision. On the one hand, you read an article from a guy who once worked on Wall Street and he says escaping your comfort zone is the right thing to do. Then you see a video on Instagram where a life coach shouts that you should be telling your comfort zone to 'go fuck itself' (charming).

On the other hand, constantly trying to escape our present situations and seeking out ways to make ourselves uncomfortable causes *more* stress, and stressed adults are proven have lower mental well-being scores, and higher levels of depression and anxiety.[23] Those aren't my claims, by the way, but the research of those crazy cats down at the Global Council on Brain Health, supported by over 20 of the world's leading neurology experts (brain doctors, to you and me).

After all, Sir Isaac Newton didn't create the concept of gravity while pulling an all-nighter, embracing cold-water plunges every morning and experimenting with extreme fasting. The foundation of his life's work was conceptualised while he was chilling out under an apple tree, and well and truly embracing his comfort zone.

This brings us to reason number two. I am not a coach, motivator, guru or teacher. In fact, the times in my life that have been my darkest – when I've felt myself spiralling out of control and had the suicide helpline on speed-dial – have been when I stepped too far out of my

22 Denning, S. (2018). How stress is the business world's silent killer. Forbes. https://www.forbes.com/sites/stephaniedenning/2018/05/04/what-is-the-cost-of-stress-how-stress-is-the-business-worlds-silent-killer/#2210311d6e06

23 Global Council on Brain Health (2018). "Brain Health and Mental Well-Being: GCBH Recommendations on Feeling Good and Functioning Well. https://www.aarp.org/content/dam/aarp/health/brain_health/2018/10/gcbh-mental-well-being-report-english.doi.10.26419-2Fpia.00037.001.pdf

comfort zone, pushed myself too hard and perceived all the great comforts in my life as 'bad things', all because that's what I was told to believe. And that's why I didn't just try to break out of my comfort zone; I planned to escape from it by jumping off a tall building.

There are so many self-styled personal-development 'experts' out there that I'm not even going to try to compete. So much has been said, written, tweeted, posted and blogged about escaping from our comfort zones already. Even if leaving our comfort zones far behind *was* the right thing to do, what could I say that hadn't already been said?

But here's the thing: what if the gurus were wrong? When escaping our comfort zones is apparently so important that thousands of people make careers out of telling us how to do it, why are people feeling more trapped than ever?

In Western society, stress levels are up. Anxiety is up. Depression is rising. Fear is creeping in. Our comfort zones are the *only* safe place we can retreat to, but what has been a safe haven for thousands of years is starting to feel like a prison.

More and more people are telling us to escape our comfort zones, face our fears and reap the rewards – but we still don't do it.

The experts aren't working.

This is what happened to me. As someone with average intelligence (i.e. I could walk and talk), I'd read, listened to and watched everything I could get my hands on to help me declare war on my poor comfort zone and escape its evil clutches forever. I lapped up information like a thirsty dog laps up water on a summer's day. Yet I still sat on my arse, day after day, telling myself excuses, making grand plans that would never be fulfilled, drinking more, arguing more and feeling more depressed than ever.

It wasn't rocket science, but I discovered there was a difference between reading about escaping my comfort zone and taking action.

Ignoring the advice of the gurus brought me Guinness World Records, Ironman and ultramarathon medals, a new career, amazing relationships, and experiences and sights beyond my wildest dreams.

My mental health improved so much that the suicide-prevention hotline even sent a delicately worded letter because they hadn't heard from me for so long and wondered if I'd finally topped myself.

I achieved all this because I realised that my comfort zone was neither an enemy nor a friend. It was not something to be wallowed in, like a jacuzzi at a Las Vegas pool party (fun at first, but if you stay too long, you're going to catch something), nor to be avoided and escaped at all costs, like a Bond villain's lair.

I discovered that our comfort zones have to be accepted. They are part of us, and they are around for a reason, like an old sweater you really should throw out but that you know you'll put on the next time you're feeling sad and need a hug.

But achieving our dreams isn't easy. In fact, it's really bloody hard. It takes pain and guts and risk and sacrifice. Whether you want to embark on a challenge; achieve a lifelong goal; make a major career change, such as moving to a new job, industry or country; try a new adventure; or simply want that amazing, unstoppable feeling of doing something you thought you couldn't do, you have to understand that you will need to leave that comfort zone behind. Don't worry, you won't be packing your bags, taking the cat, slamming the door and saying goodbye forever; you're just going to another place. Your comfort zone will be there waiting for you when you need it, and, believe me, you *will*.

The place you're visiting is different. It will mean going on a journey and taking your mind quite literally somewhere it hasn't been before. It will involve change, it will feel a bit weird, and it definitely won't be easy. But once you make the commitment and decide to go there, the rewards can be life-changing.

The place you are going to is the *conquer* zone.

The beauty of the conquer zone is that anyone can take their mind there. You don't need to spend a shit-ton of money, and it isn't only for athletes, corporate highflyers, the young, the old, the privileged elite or the dirt poor. All you need to get there is an ounce of determination and the ability to dream.

I'm strange (in so many ways, so I've been told). Statistically, I should still be in my box of an office, doing shit I hated for money I spent on every vice imaginable. I should have still been saying to myself, "Everyone has a dream, but it will never happen," or "No one is supposed to enjoy what they do; that's life." I should have done what normal people do by getting over the sudden death of a loved one and going back to so-called 'normal'.

However, when I took a different path to my conquer zone, I discovered a life from a story book. I jumped out of helicopters and stared down the throat of great white sharks. I sank to my knees in the middle of the Sahara Desert with only a million stars for company. I jumped through race finish lines, and I pushed my body until it broke and bled.

I was able to do all these things as a 'normal person' who just didn't want to be *quite* so normal any more. And the real beauty of this approach – the final, golden piece of the jigsaw puzzle – is that I *didn't* have to abandon my comfort zone to do it. My comfort zone and I are still good friends, we still see each other regularly, and I bloody love it.

Now you understand the truth about our comfort zones: the history, the good, the bad and the reasons why they protect us yet also hinder our chances of success (like the time my mum accompanied me to a school disco when I was 15). But it's time to take a different path.

In the next chapters, I'm going to set out what you need to do to enter your conquer zone.

You're going to need to identify the tipping point at which you decide enough is enough.

You're going to recognise there is no time like the present.

You'll learn how to prepare in the right way for something you once considered impossible.

You'll realise motivation is only part of the process, and you'll know how to take action and achieve whatever it is you're trying to conquer.

And then we'll talk about what happens when it all goes tits up.

Let's go forth and conquer.

FOUR

RETURN OF THE JFDI

"You can't make decisions based on fear and the possibility of what might happen."

Michelle Obama

"Daddy, you never do anything exciting." The words of my six-year-old son cut through me like a knife. *How*, I wondered, *do the most innocent of humans, who are unburdened by the thoughts, fears and mental baggage of adults, manage to say the most hurtful of things?*

When a child says something so simple yet so devastatingly truthful to us, we may smile, laugh it off, and come up with an excuse about time, money or work. But when we are lying in bed at night, those words return like a ghost in the darkness, reminding us of the decisions we postponed or the actions we never took.

On any other day, I could have accepted that my son had a fair point. After all, back when I had no idea my conquer zone existed, he would have been right. He would have heard me discussing my grand plans at the dinner table: plans we all knew would never amount to anything. We would have walked hand in hand through the woods, talking excitedly about challenges to accomplish and sensational places to visit. Then, as the imposing tree trunks surrounded me like the bars of a prison, and the leaves and branches looked sternly down upon me like an emerald glass ceiling preventing my dreams from rising up to the heavens, I would turn to him and say: "Maybe one day we'll do all these things. One day. Maybe. You never know."

But this time was different, and it's fair to say I was more than a little pissed off by the words springing from my little cherub's mouth. Because, at the very moment he was accusing me of never doing anything exciting with my life, he was holding something in his hands. The shimmer of gold escaped between the gaps in his fingers and reflected off his face, making him appear like a tomb raider who had just discovered and prised open an ancient treasure chest. A red ribbon was entwined around his wrist, and he twirled one end absently around his tiny hand as if it were prayer beads.

While the apple of my eye was accusing me of being a boring old bastard, he was toying with my medal from the Marathon des Sables. This was the medal I had earned eight months earlier while dragging my dehydrated, broken and bleeding body across 200 miles of Saharan Desert.

Irony clearly wasn't on the school curriculum this term.

"*Oh, don't I?*" I spluttered. "You know that's not exactly a drinks coaster you're playing with."

"I know," he replied in that amazingly simple manner children possess, which enables them to cut through bullshit and get straight to the point. "But that was *last year*, Daddy. You need to keep doing exciting things."

"Oh, must I? And I suppose you have something in mind?"

"Yes, Daddy, I do. I want you to break a world record."

And five short weeks later I was standing on the start line of the 2019 Liverpool Marathon, dressed as a fisherman. Sweating in my head-to-toe, waterproof, bright-yellow outfit, with my arm already aching from the 3kg fishing box in my hand, and my feet starting to protest and swell in my rubber wellington boots, I stood out like an amber distress flair in a sea of Lycra and toned flesh. Only two thoughts went through my mind:

1. *I should have bought him a PlayStation for Christmas instead of the sodding* Guinness World Records *book.*
2. *This could very well have been the worst decision I have ever made.*

The traditional approach to motivating people to step outside their comfort zones begins with a compelling statement such as "The hardest thing to do is to decide and take action." I can say with some authority, it is not. The hardest thing to do is to run 26.2 miles in rubber boots, especially when your toenails fell off around mile 10, and the flesh of both your heels has been rubbed away to the bone when you're still three miles from the finish line.

Making the decision to *begin*, however, is by far the most important thing. Equally as important is the decision to *keep going*.

Although I didn't realise it at the time, the decision I took when sitting on my son's bedroom floor, while he employed his tactic of talking about everything and nothing to postpone going to bed, was a huge turning point in my life.

As I still bore the physical and mental scars from my sandy jolly in the Sahara Desert the year before – as well as the immense pride and sense of achievement – it would be fair to say that my comfort zone and I had got to know each other a bit too well again. Like two illicit lovers who hook up and promise themselves it will be 'just the once' before embarking on a complex double-life built upon a web of lies, I only had eyes for my comfort zone; however, my conquer zone was sitting in the lost recesses of my mind night after night, hoping and waiting desperately for me to call.

But I decided I couldn't lie to myself and dine out on that monumental expedition forever. The trouser waistlines were getting tighter again, and, more worryingly, the creeping dark claws of mental anxiety were starting to dig into my brain.

Deciding to break a Guinness World Record was a call to action: I told my comfort zone that we needed some time apart, and I plucked up the courage to turn up at my conquer zone's house with some flowers and beg for forgiveness.

But with over 40,000 Guinness World Records in existence, which one should I break? Running felt instinctively like the right choice. I knew I wasn't good at much, but I wasn't bad at putting one foot in front of the other. Breaking any actual distance records was out of the question. Try as I might, no amount of positive thinking was going to transform me from a 37-year-old management consultant into a 25-year-old Olympian from Kenya.

As luck would have it, the London Marathon was broadcast on TV later that day. My children pointed joyfully at the many colourful characters and costumes, while I slumped back on the sofa. I recalled my very first marathon, in London in 2012. You may not think it's impossible to run a marathon without leaving your comfort zone, but I can assure you it is.

My build-up to that first, fateful marathon had involved drinking heavily, eating crap and developing a fondness for Marlboro-flavoured training supplements. On a couple of occasions, I even paused my training runs to sit on a wall and spark up a cig. *It will help your lungs adjust to the exertions*, my comfort zone whispered to me, like a doctor from the 1920s. I had approached that race with arrogance and incompetence; although I had decided to challenge myself, I hadn't bothered to make any positive decisions regarding my lifestyle, and my conquer zone was so scared of me that it didn't even bother to make itself known. This is resulted in my very first marathon handing me damaged ligaments, shit-stained underwear, busted knees and a kicked arse.

As I winced at the memory, I was reminded that it is never a good idea to take the piss out of a marathon. But now – urged on by my children as their bright, little eyes widened while watching the event on TV – I was going to run a marathon dressed as a bloody fisherman (not a fisherman covered in blood – well, I hoped not at least).

Why a fisherman? Well, my children loved the sea, and I wanted to raise awareness of the damage humans are doing to the oceans: plastics, pollution, overfishing, whaling and dumping of toxic waste. As I see it, we have no right to royally fuck up another creature's habitat, especially when those creatures can't have their say. My hometown of Liverpool was also a proud maritime city (there's always lots of talk about trade and being the gateway to the world, although the whole slavery thing seems to get brushed under the carpet these days).

Another reason behind my choice was the record for running a marathon in a bikini is two hours and 53 minutes, and I knew I had no hope of beating that.

My decision made, I sent off my application to Guinness World Records...

And then totally forgot about it. But the part that matters is that I actually *decided* to make it happen. I *could* have patted my kids on the head, and made some bullshit excuse about work or time. I *could* have promised to undertake the challenge at some unspecified point in the future, switched over to *Peppa Pig* and hoped they forgot about it. I *could* have just said no, I was perfectly happy in my comfort zone, and there was no financial, logical or emotional reason to shift towards my conquer zone one little bit.

But a tiny part of me wondered, *What if?* What if I could show my kids it was possible to achieve anything they put their minds to? What if I could raise some money for a local charity at the same time? What if I could put a smile on people's faces? What if I could take a leap into my conquer zone and prove to myself that I could do things I never once considered possible?

Fired-up on energy and emotion, I opened the email from the Guinness World Records team: I had been accepted.

I shat myself. (Not literally, although such an unfortunate episode did happen during that first marathon in 2012).

At a point that marked a new chapter in my life – an instance that should have been filled with passion, excitement and inspiration – I felt only one emotion: fear.

Immediately, my comfort zone started to bang on the insides of my skull, turning the volume up and shouting excuses like a drunken neighbour when the police arrive.

"You won't be able to do it.

You're not fit enough.

You're not prepared enough.

You can defer until next year.

No one knows your record attempt has been approved, so you can just delete the email and they'll forget about it eventually."

My comfort zone's rowdy protests were absolutely correct. All I had to do to make these objections a reality was to listen and obey. But there was a second voice, a much calmer, quieter whisper. It was my conquer zone: *What if you did it?*

I visualised the looks on my children's faces when I crossed the finish line. I imagined the cheers of the crowd; the money I could raise for charity; the good I could do to start making up for some of the shitty, drunken mistakes of my past; and how I could perhaps show others that anything is possible once you enter your conquer zone.

There was no going back now. I had decided once, and I decided again: it was time to commit. Then I scrolled to the bottom of the email and devoured the confusing array of extremely detailed, highly specific, rules and regulations:

Yellow hat – *fine.*

Yellow waterproof trousers and jacket – *feels a bit sadomasochistic and sweaty, but OK then.*

A 3kg fishing box – a *bit heavy, but whatever.*

Then I saw it: "The competitor must wear knee-high, rubber wellington boots for the entirety of the record attempt."

A marathon wearing wellies. Shit.

I hadn't expected this sting in the tail. I'd assumed I could wear my faithful running trainers, the very shoes that had carried me across marathon finishing lines before. But not this time.

Once you make a decision – once you pass that point of worrying, deliberating and overthinking, and actually *decide* – it's amazing how many so-called 'experts' appear out of the woodwork like rats from a sewer. Safe and secure in their zones of comfort, friends, colleagues and complete strangers would morph suddenly into the world's leading experts on running a marathon dressed as an extra from a fetish movie.

On learning of my challenge, one colleague in particular would lean back in his chair and give that long, satisfied sigh of a person who believes they are the oracle of all knowledge. In his mind's eye, he was Yoda, and I was a young Luke Skywalker, who had sought out his wisdom on how to use the Force. He reached his hands behind his head, exposing the moist, yellowing sweat patches in the armpits of his shirt, and lifted one scuffed shoe up onto his desk, causing his trousers to tighten around the crotch area, which he was pointing in my direction. It was like he was preparing for his centrefold in *Middle-Aged Businessman Quarterly* (*MABQ*, available on subscription):

MABQ: "Yeah, what you want to do, Freddie, is cut the soles out of the welly boots so you can fit them over your trainers."

Me: "Hmm, thanks for that, but I think it's classified as cheating."

MABQ: "Nah, mate, it's just called 'playing the game'. Also, don't worry about that costume bollocks, just change out of it after the first mile and put it back on again before the finish."

Me: "I'm not sure that's allowed either." I made a mental note to get him some deodorant in the next Secret Santa.

MABQ: "Bullshit! You need to make life as easy as possible for yourself, my son."

Me: "It's all about setting myself a challenge… doing something that has never been done before." I tried desperately to look anywhere but at his crotch, which was now close enough to be classified as a lap dance.

MABQ: "What the actual fuck? What training plan are you following?"

For the next five minutes, he continued to lecture me on training plans ("waste of fucking time"), running shoes ("need to be expensive") and race strategy ("have a shit in a bush if you need to"). I smiled and nodded while trying not to look at the spreading dampness beneath his arms or the groin that squirmed like a squirrel trapped in a sack.

Before making my excuses and walking away, I couldn't help but ask one more question – *Columbo* style:

Me: "Oh, by the way, how many marathons have you run?"
MABQ: "*Running?* Fucking waste of time, mate; it's bad for the knees. Humans were designed to sit on the sofa."

Walking away from this disturbing episode, I realised something: the decision to challenge yourself is sometimes the easiest thing to do. The hard part is *sticking* to that decision when the world is saying you are wrong.

FISHING FOR COMPLIMENTS

What the fuck am I doing?

It wasn't the first time I'd asked myself that question over the last few days. The past 48 hours had brought rollercoaster of emotions: the highs of confidence, self-belief and determination, followed by the plummeting, stomach-churning lows of fear, weakness and doubt. But all rides must come to an end sometime, and now it was the moment of truth.

As I stood on the start line of the Liverpool Marathon – a fishing box clasped tightly in my hand, and sweat oozing from the rim of my yellow rubber sou'wester and running down my face – I could feel a thousand pairs of eyes upon me. The looks from my fellow competitors ranged from amazement and amusement to disbelief and pity. I tried to ignore the whispered comments passed through hand-cupped mouths, the eye-rolls and the shaking of heads. I attempted to close my ears to the words floating on the early morning breeze: "not a hope in hell," "bloody ridiculous," and, "not a clue what's about to hit him."

I wanted the ground to swallow me up. What had started off as a bit of a laugh to impress my kids, challenge my limits and raise some money for a local charity had become suddenly very serious. I looked down at my constricting black rubber boots and fought back tears. *Why can't people be more supportive? I thought others might have been inspired, but they just think I'm stupid. Why does everyone have to be so bloody* mean *to each other?*

I desperately wanted the taunts and ridicule to stop. Then, as the sun started to shine more brightly through the low mist that had blanketed the Liverpool docks, a revelation hit me: the jeers, the mocking and the harsh words from others – they would never stop. I had no control over what other people thought about me or said about my challenge.

In fact, they were probably right.

I *did* look bloody ridiculous.

I probably *didn't* have a hope in hell.

I didn't have a clue regarding what was about to happen.

I couldn't help but smile at that last insult. My preparation for the record attempt hadn't been ideal. In fact, I'd never run more than a mile in the fisherman's outfit before the race. A week earlier, I had pulled on the rubber boots, dressed in the yellow clothing, grabbed my fishing box and attempted a run through some local woods. Half a mile later, I was feeling pretty pleased with myself, until I met Doris.

Doris was an elderly lady, a grandmother to two children, who enjoyed a quiet, peaceful life and loved a nice walk with her little dog, Pebbles, through the woods every morning. On this fateful day, however, Doris and Pebbles' peaceful stroll was shattered by a panting hooligan dressed in yellow sprinting towards her.

Imagine, if you will (as I have done on many sleepless nights), that you are a frail, old lady minding her own business, enjoying the company of your little furry friend and listening to the birds. The next thing you know, a man wearing black rubber boots, and dressed as what can only be described as a cross between a serial killer from a slasher movie and the world's shittest stripper comes charging towards you carrying a big, heavy box. What would run through your mind?

Death. Death was foremost in Doris' thoughts at the moment. She stopped and stared at me, paralysed in terror and certain these were the final moments of her life.

After I had stopped and apologised to Doris and Pebbles, reassured her that I was neither a serial killer nor a stripper, and made sure she wasn't going to drop dead from a heart attack, I had trotted home quickly. With only the flap-flap sound of my boots hitting the pavement to keep me company, I decided to keep my fisherman's outfit under wraps until race-day.

The urgent roar of an air horn tore me from my daydream. The race had started. I continued to look at the floor as I shuffled forwards, carried along in a crowd of bodies buzzing with nervous energy. Still, I tried to duck and hide, though attempting to be as inconspicuous as possible is difficult when you're six feet tall and look like a walking IKEA logo. As the fear, claustrophobia and pure shame squeezed me like a vice, tightening my chest and causing me to gasp for breath, I knew something had to change. If it didn't, I was going to have a panic attack, escape the crowd and quit this challenge before it had even begun.

So I made a decision.

I decided I could let the taunts, the insults, the sly smiles and the pointed fingers win, or I could decide to show these running bros the middle finger, say fuck the lot of them and give it my best shot. After all, everybody thought I was going to fail. I could just say, "They're right," and let it happen, or could I decide to prove them wrong and create my own future. Success was far from guaranteed, but I could damn well give it a try.

As I crossed the start line, I lifted my chin and smiled at the world. I decided to embrace this challenge; no matter how hard things got, no matter how much pain I was in, and no matter if I failed or succeeded,

I was going to own it. I lifted my feet, took a deep breath and strode forwards to greatness.

A mile later, I knew I was in serious fucking trouble. *Why the hell was I doing this to myself?*

The rubber boots gripped my legs like a trap, getting tighter by the second as my feet started to protest and swell. I tried to hide my worries by plastering a thin grin on my face, waving madly at the people in the crowd who looked at me, turned away and then doing a double take as their brains processed what their eyes had just witnessed. They looked at me with that bewildered, head-at-an-angle-and-mouth-open pose: the same expression a child visiting a zoo might have when the daddy elephant climbs on top of the mummy elephant.

On the outside, I was smiling, but, internally, I was already worried. When I saw my family at mile two, I paused to plant a sweaty kiss on the foreheads of my children, but locked eyes with my wife. "This isn't looking good," I muttered.

"*Falling apart already?* Get yourself moving then!" she replied with a total lack of sympathy as she shoved me in the back to move me on my way.

Later, my children would tell me that Mummy, Granny and Grandpa had seen the expression on my face and realised I wasn't going to make it. They were already devising strategies to console me when failure inevitably struck.

As I plodded through the hills of Liverpool's metropolitan centre, which rose steeply from the docks and the River Mersey, it felt as if shards of glass were being forced into my feet. Every step was starting to become agony. The only distraction from the pain was the slightly less painful sensation of rivers of sweat running into my eyes. I kept switching the 3kg fishing box from hand to hand, trying yet failing to find an angle that would allow me to hold the container with a degree of comfort while pumping my arms to build some momentum into my stride.

Propelling myself forwards was already a concern. Momentum would give me pace, pace would allow me to eat up some distance in a shorter time, and time would give me the world record. The simple race strategy I had devised in my head was to run a mile every 10 minutes. So, 26 miles at 10 minutes a mile would mean completing the marathon in 260 minutes (or 4 hours and 20 minutes) and therefore breaking the world record by a monumental 25 minutes. When I considered a good day's race to involve a pace of a mile every seven and a half minutes, I thought this was achievable. Until I started running dressed as a yellow duck mixed with a sex toy, that is.

As I reached the peaks of the hills surrounding Liverpool, I ran around the iconic Everton and Liverpool football stadiums, and through the sprawling greenery of Stanley Park, the pain continued to grow throughout my limbs. On reaching the outskirts of some decidedly dodgy housing estates, where excited revellers cheered me on as I strode through clouds of cigarette smoke, with half-drunk beer cans crunching under my feet, a new sensation started to grow.

It began as an absent, wobbling sensation inside my socks. The feeling took me back to my childhood and wearing a pair of second-hand shoes, which were polished to look like new but being held together with bits of superglue and pure faith. Below my ankles, something was falling apart; I just didn't know what it was. Panicking that my boots were about to give up on me and leave the record attempt in tatters, I allowed myself a five-second pause to inspect my footwear. I could see nothing untoward. Everything seemed to be one piece on the outside, but, as I resumed my agonising trot forwards, the rattling began again. It was almost as if my children had slipped a small coin inside each of my socks, and the hard piece of metal was slowly working its way around inside the fabric of the material, nibbling and jarring against the skin of my toes.

When the realisation hit me, I was calmer than I expected. I could have decided to panic, to call for help, or to sit down on the pavement and cry. But I knew this would mean my efforts would be for nothing. There was no bravery, no inspirational mental dialogue from my conquer zone telling me that pain was just fear leaving the body. I simply gave a tiny shrug of my yellow shoulders and accepted the situation that had been presented to me: one by one, like a row of collapsing dominoes, my toenails were falling off.

I had 18 miles to go.

But my bleeding, naked toes became trivial compared to another growing threat I faced: time. No matter how fast I strode or how high I attempted to lift my feet, my pace was plummeting like a politician's approval ratings during COVID-19. Nine minutes per mile; nine minutes 45 seconds; 10 minutes 10 seconds; 11 minutes; then 11 minutes 15 seconds. Despite shouting and crying and begging and praying, my body started to hold up its hands and say *enough is enough*.

Shuddering in pain with every step, I ran back through the city. The unseeing bronze eyes of John, Paul, Ringo and George looked upon me as I ran hobbled past the Beatles statue, muttering under my breath that I looked like I belonged on a fucking yellow submarine. As smooth pavement gave way to the cobblestones of Chinatown, with the uneven bricks rolling before me like grey scales across a dragon's back, a voice inside me became louder than the cheering crowd.

It was my comfort zone.

"You've had enough," it said. *"You're going to fail."* As soon as I tuned in and started to listen, the excuses came tumbling out of my mind like rats from a sinking ship: *"Don't risk injury; You can try again next year; Everybody fails; At least you raised some money for charity;"* and *"At least you tried."*

Resigned to my fate, I half-sat, half-collapsed onto the pavement and set my fishing box gently down beside me. I leaned back and watched the procession of runners striding past, a mixture of pity and laugher across their sweat-strewn faces as they looked down on the fisherman whose prize had got away.

As I shrugged, blew out my cheeks and reached down to pull off my boots, a tingle of excitement sped through me as I relished the waves of relief resulting from the removal of my footwear. However, as I grabbed hold of the boot and tugged, a new wave of agony flashed through my body, as if I had shoved my toes into an electric socket. As the shreds of nerves attached to my toenails tugged, blood-filled blisters burst and sodden flesh was ripped from muscle, the realisation hit me that I wasn't just going to kick off my footwear and put my feet up in front of the fire. In some kind of delicious irony, it seemed that the only thing causing me more pain than running in these boots was removing them.

Not for the first time that morning, I had a decision to make. My comfort zone didn't even bloody care about my bloody feet any more. I could just lie on my back, relishing the cold hardness of the pavement, not thinking nor caring about how I would get up or get home. After all, if I looked pathetic enough for long enough, someone was bound to come to my aid.

Or, I could entertain the thoughts of my conquer zone.

These wisps of ponderings and fragments of speculation were not particularly motivational. I just allowed the conquer zone to cut through the emotions of pain and fear and to tell me the facts: there was only one way to get these damned boots off my feet, and that was to finish this fucking race.

As I realised what I was about to do, I yelled out in frustration. Rolling on to my stomach, then rising up to a kneeling position and, finally, dragging myself up onto my feet, like the rusting tinman from the Wizard of Oz, I berated myself for my stupidity. *Why had I decided to do this? Why couldn't I just decide to quit?* I thought about why I'd even chosen to do this challenge: showing my kids their dad wasn't a one-trick pony, helping a local charity and giving people something to smile about in a world where the only news seemed to be bad. Setting forwards once more, I gritted my teeth, shut out my complaining comfort zone and tried to hear my conquer zone spur me on quietly: *"You're still breathing, so you're still winning."*

*

Twenty-two miles completed. The open parkland and majestically wide, tree-lined walkways, which could have doubled as a location for *Downton Abbey* were providing little distraction. I wasn't winning at all. I was failing – and I was fucked.

As I continued my stagger around the historic Sefton Park, past the ornate lake and angular palm house, jutting out of the grass like a shard of glass, one thing was burdening me more than the fishing box, which had somehow transformed long ago into a box of bricks: the weight of failure was pressing down upon me.

I couldn't recall exactly when it happened – maybe at mile 15, maybe mile 18 or perhaps, deep down, I'd known right from the start – but now failure was staring me in the face. I hadn't been able to pick up the pace, and looked helplessly at my watch again and again, hoping the numbers tauntingly displayed on its screen were wrong. But I knew they weren't. What made this growing sense of failure even worse, however, was that – as I tried to run the sums in my broken, clouded mind – I realised I was going to miss out on the world record by a matter of minutes.

In a twisted way, I would have preferred it if my failure had been spectacular: a sprained ankle, perhaps, or fainting from heat exhaustion. Nothing too life-threatening, obviously; the days of wishing myself serious harm, or worse, were long gone. But on this day, with failure taunting me and my comfort zone holding up a big middle finger and a sign saying "Told You So", all I wanted was for this race to blow up in my face so I could pack up my fishing box and go home for dinner.

As I trudged past the sign for mile 23, I contemplated success being so agonisingly, painstakingly out of reach. So close but yet so far. "*You just weren't good enough.*" A weird half-cry, half-yelp of panic escaped from my throat. I imagined the disappointed faces of my children, friends, sponsors and everyone who had helped me get to this moment. I could imagine the pats on the back, the heads tilted to one side in sympathy and the pursed lips. "*At least you gave it a try.*"

My body had become so dehydrated by this stage; all the sweat I had perspired was trapped by the heavy, polyester jacket and trousers, causing my clothing to become a miniature, yellow greenhouse. Objects in my vision swam and floated like wraiths atop a misty sea, my head pounded, and my parched lips cracked and bled. Glancing down at my watch, I noticed that the veins in my wrist were protruding like writhing snakes beneath my skin. On seeing my pace, my heart sank further, I was now running barely a mile every 13 minutes – way too slow.

Something sparked in my brain.

My running speed was on its arse, but when I looked at my total time, I felt a faint glimmer of hope cut through the darkness. I had crossed the start line four hours and five minutes earlier, which meant the world record was alive for another 40 minutes. Three miles in 40 minutes. A parkrun in just under an episode of *Suits*.

Could I?

When I reflected on this moment of truth, I remembered how strange it was to be so alone. As I contemplated whether to decide to plod on, embrace a spirited defeat, or bet the farm (and my feet) and go for broke, I was totally by myself. At that particular, distant point on the marathon route, no spectators lined the streets, nor were any runners in sight ahead of or behind me. It felt like I was alone on the earth, with a decision to make that would alter how I viewed any future trial, tribulation, adventure or challenge.

As my comfort and conquer zones fought another duel of willpower, I looked up at the overcast sky and asked myself a question: "*If you quit now, could you, with all your heart, say you gave it everything today? Have you cried? Have you vomited? Have you crawled on your hands and knees until they bled? Have you exhausted every single possible shred of hope and opportunity?*"

I realised I had not.

Admittedly, I had cried and bled, but I hadn't vomited down my delightful yellow outfit yet. *Every cloud, and all that.*

In quick succession, another flash hit me: *You're down, you're out, you're bleeding and you're broken. You're cut to pieces and fucked up.*

But…this is as bad as it gets.

I realised there were no more tears to cry. I had nothing left to lose. Literally, because, at this point, I was sure all my toenails had fallen off. This time there was no bravado, no roar of anger and no rallying cry. I simply lifted my head and decided. Enough was enough; I had spent so many years self-sabotaging and running away from the faintest hint of success. Today, I was going to run towards it.

"Just fucking do it, Freddie. JFDI."

The headwind blew in from the Irish Sea and charged up the River Mersey like an express train, battering my face and trying to blow me off balance. I put my head down and surged forwards. The plop-plopping of my rubber boots on the ground had been replaced by a sucking, squelching sound that reminded me of long-forgotten days playing in the woods with my father, and our feet sinking into the deep mud. In that final mile, I wanted so desperately to feel his spirit, and to know he was watching and guiding me to the finish with a proud smile upon his face. I knew, however, if he were watching me flail and stumble back to Liverpool's Albert Dock, he would be shaking his head and muttering, "Why, you foolish bastard?"

In the final 200 metres, as the vomit rose in my throat, and I bounced off barriers and kerbstones as if replaying the darkest, most drunken nights from my past, the thunderous crowd brought me to my senses. Reinvigorated, I found a strength I had always wondered if I possessed but assumed had been lost and abandoned long ago. Wanting desperately to look at my watch and check my time, but fearing what it might tell me, I tried to search for my loved ones in the throng of spectators. In the blur of faces, noise and colour, I locked eyes with my wife. With what felt like explosions detonating inside my mind, I couldn't comprehend her words, but I got the gist of it: *"I love you; now fucking run, dickhead."*

20 metres to go. My vision turned grey, and the roaring grew in my ears as if I had descended into a deep, dark tunnel. Saliva flooded into my parched mouth, and I shivered as a new river of sweat ran down my spine.

You're going down. Fast.

My knees buckled and started to give way as I tried to lift a trembling hand, desperately willing the finish line to come to me. As my hope evaporated, I felt something clasp my shaking palm. I glanced downwards and saw my eldest son's hand in mine.

"Come ON, Daddy!" he yelled.

As my heart flooded with love and determination, I glanced across and saw Luke, my youngest son, beside me. He too had climbed over the crowd barriers to help to bring his father home.

As I crossed the finish line flanked by my two sons, I collapsed onto the ground. Shaking with pain and exhaustion, I was attacked by a swarm of kisses and hugs. At that moment, I realised that they did not care whether their father had been successful or not. All that mattered to them was that I had decided to try and then decided never to quit.

Rising unsteadily to my feet and bracing myself against the fresh wave of pain surging through my body, I heard the loudspeakers announce the words I'd dreamed about for so long: "Freddie Bennett, you are a Guinness World Record breaker!"

CTRL-ALT-DELETE

Our lives are an endless string of decisions – some are trivial ("Americano or push the boat out and get a flat white?") and others are life-changing ("Is now the right time to quit my job and book that journey to South America?"). It is something of an irony that, when our comfort zones have become more difficult to escape than ever, comfort has provided us with more choice-related anxiety, not less.

Our comfort zones have swamped our lives to such an extent that most of us now suffer from what American psychologist Barry Schwartz calls 'the paradox of choice'.[24] This is the processes whereby

24 Schwartz, Barry. (2004) *The paradox of choice : why more is less*

making a decision becomes overwhelming due to the many potential outcomes and risks that may result from making the 'wrong choice'.

Essentially, our brains are like the computers from 20 years ago: a massive monitor sitting atop a big box containing all the chips and circuits and a slow-loading screen for Windows 2000. Ask the computer to open a spreadsheet, and everything works fine. Maybe you turn things up a notch and turn on the screeching, ear-bleeding electronic jumble of a dial-up modem; it's no problem. The computer's brain is reviewing data, making calculations and completing tasks.

But then you start to get comfortable and demand more of your machine. You open a Word document; visit the website of a weird little book-selling start-up called 'Amazon'; while you're waiting an eternity for the page to load, you fire up a game of Doom; and then a friend pings you on MSN Messenger, asking a question about your history homework, so you put your Encarta CD-ROM (look it up, kids) into the computer's disk drive.

Before you know it, your trusty, dusty computer has crashed. It crashed because you were asking too much of it. Its silicon brain could not handle the vast array of decisions you demanded it make. It didn't know what task to prioritise or what outcome to achieve; all it realised was its little mechanical mind was spinning too fast and it hadn't a clue what to do next – so it froze. Then the only action we could take was to press ctrl-alt-delete to reset the thing and start again.

Our organic brains work in much the same way, and we encounter examples of the paradox of choice every day:

- The person frozen like a statue, open mouthed, staring up at the Starbucks menu.
- The supermarket shopper whose trolley crashed into your ankles as they were walking aimlessly down the aisle while struggling to comprehend how many rolls of toilet paper they should buy.
- The distracted mobile phone user who walks into a lamppost while sending a WhatsApp message, composing an Instagram

post and watching a hilarious cat video on Facebook, all at the same time.

No matter how fit, rich, good-looking or intelligent we are (or not in my case), one thing can barely change: the amount of information our brains can take in at any one time.

This is also backed up by science. In 2004, two psychology academics named Christopher Chabris and Daniel Simons devised an experiment called 'the invisible gorilla'.[25]* This study involved showing a group of people a video in which six people – three in white shirts and three in black shirts – pass a basketball around for 80 seconds. The viewer is asked to count in their heads the number of passes made by the people in white shirts. While the basketball action unfurls, a gorilla walks into the picture, thumps its chest and then walks off after spending nine seconds on screen.

Even when viewers were given advance warning that this would happen, half of them failed to spot the gorilla. Perhaps the individuals who took part in this experiment were just a bit short-sighted, thick, lazy, preoccupied or unobservant? Maybe, but they were also all students at Harvard University.

The experiment tells us two things about the decisions we make and the lives of comfort we live in. Firstly, we are usually too caught up in our own struggles and decisions to notice much of what is going on around us. Secondly, half the time, we don't realise what we are missing out on, even if someone gives us a head's up beforehand.

When it comes to those big, crazy, scary, challenging decisions, they have a way of creeping around the corners of our conscience and stealing into our everyday thoughts. This is why, when we are mulling over whether to embark on any type of big challenge, it feels so damn hard to concentrate.

Going back to the evolutionary story, our caveman and cavewoman brains liked to keep our decisions simple: Hungry? *Eat.* Scared? *Run or*

---

25   Chabris, C. F., & Simons, D. J. (2010). *The invisible gorilla: And other ways our intuitions deceive us.* New York: Crown.

*   Try it yourself. Don't forget to say hello to the gorilla. http://www.theinvisiblegorilla. com

fight. Tired? *Sleep*. Expand the human race? *Jump in the back of the cave with a friend and pull the mammoth-fur curtain across for some privacy.*

But, thanks to our comfort zones, we have so much extra shit going on in our brains that it makes it more difficult to compartmentalise our thoughts. This is why we spend our work meetings wondering whether we should enter that marathon or not, spend our showers debating whether we should book that kitesurfing lesson, and watch Netflix while scrolling through our phones and contemplating why our lives didn't quite turn out as we imagined.

And then, just like that Windows 2000 PC, we freeze. This period of suspension may last for a few seconds, but it can last for years or even a lifetime. This means when that moment comes and we realise it's time to press ctrl-alt-delete and reset our minds, it may be too late. The opportunity may have passed, and the decision we were dwelling on for so long – the judgement that took up so much energy that it prevented us from functioning properly – is no longer relevant any more. While we were frozen and taking an eternity to decide, life carried on without us, and the opportunity came and went. On the journey of our lives, we were too busy staring out the window, deliberating whether to take the path into the unknown that could dramatically change our course. Then, all of a sudden, we have travelled past it, and we are forever staring at it in our rear-view mirror, wondering what might have been.

How often have you weighed up whether to buy something or not, only to find it had then sold out?

How many times did you deliberate whether to do something or not, then finally decided only to have COVID-19 hit and make all your plans for 2020 null and void?

How many hours of your life have you wasted debating something over and over in your head, such that the pain of the decision-making process has clouded the enjoyment of the event itself?

I have encountered the aforementioned frustrations on enough occasions to fill a thousand lifetimes. Each and every time, I would throw my hands up in frustration and give myself a psychological beating for making my life so difficult. *"Why can't you just bloody decide?"* After all, the YouTube videos had told me to just decide and make it happen, the books had told me to feel the fear and do it anyway, and the podcasts encouraged me to jump into the unknown.

But I was still paralysed by indecision. If anything, I was suffering from a paradox of self-help choice. I had also discovered a cunning distraction method: Do you have a massive, life-changing decision to make? Go and watch a couple of TED (technology, entertainment, design) talks! This way, you can waste half an hour, safe in your comfort zone, telling yourself this is part of your 'journey', when all you are doing in reality is delaying taking action. But, hey, at least you're lying on the sofa looking at your phone, so life can't be bad! Not bad at all, in fact; extremely *comfortable*.

However, on the occasion of the Liverpool Marathon, I ultimately decided to step towards my conquer zone and made the decision to break a world record; against all the better judgements of safety, sanity, risk and time – I took a different approach.

I didn't wait for my brain to go into overload before pressing ctrl-alt-delete. I understood my goals and motivations. Rather than seeing the decision-making process as a crazy bit of prehistoric psychology sprinkled with a dusting of modern-day midlife crisis, I embraced it and sought to understand it. In my comfort zone, decision-making had been a no-go topic, like discussing religion or Brexit at a dinner party. For me to enter my conquer zone, I knew I would have to grab that decision-making process, kill it and serve it up for the main course.

THE BATTLEGROUND

Conflict is in our nature, from the early days when we realised sticks and stones could break our bones; through *Game of Thrones*-style swords and shields; to bullets, bombs and cyber warfare. Most of us, however, face a different kind of battle every day: the struggle taking place between our comfort and conquer zones.

Generally, we tend to make rational decisions. Every time we weigh up the options, and go with the safe bet, minimise our risks, and generally choose the path of least resistance, this is our comfort zone telling us to do the 'normal' thing.

If we are caught between two options, say, whether to spend the day playing with the kids and then watching a movie, or dressing up as a fisherman, running a marathon and scarring ourselves for life, we tend to review the pros and cons of each and then trust our comfortable, rational minds to give us the right answer. And the beauty of this process is that we'll tell ourselves we made the 'sensible' choice and give our comfort zones a little high-five while we settle into the sofa.

But our comfort zone is – unsurprisingly – very lazy when it comes to decision-making. All that rational thinking and playing it safe takes up a lot of energy. This is why people turn into zombies when looking at the Starbucks menu or fail to see a gorilla staring them in the face.

However, our conquer zones make decisions in a totally different way. Conquer-zone thoughts are rapid, powerful and reactive. These types of decisions come from a deeper, more primal place within our minds. They are our impulses, urges and desires. Conquer-zone decisions are also known as our *gut instincts*.

Professor Daniel Kahneman from Princeton University and his colleague Amos Tversky at the Hebrew University of Jerusalem and Stanford University first developed the theory that we have these two different ways of approaching decisions. Those risk-taking radicals at the Royal Swedish Academy of Sciences must have thought the pair were on to something, as their work was awarded the Nobel Prize for Economics in 2002.[26]

Why were Kahneman and Tversky awarded a Nobel Prize in Economics and not one for something such as psychology? Well, firstly, it turns out there is no Nobel Prize for psychology (that's three hours of my life spent internet researching that I'll never get back),

---

26   The Sveriges Riksbank Prize in Economic Sciences in Memory of Alfred Nobel 2002. https://www.nobelprize.org/prizes/economic-sciences/2002/summary/

and, secondly, much of the conflict between our comfort and conquer zones comes back to one of our favourite Western influences: money.

Let's have a look at an example. Say you're presented with a challenge that's something difficult but not impossible, and is highly emotionally and spiritually rewarding. Climbing Kilimanjaro perhaps or an opportunity to walk the Inca Trail. More likely than not, it will be your conquer zone that fires up first. When presented with an option that could quite rightly be called 'the opportunity of a lifetime', most people would give an instinctive response along the lines of, "Wow, that would be amazing." (Apart from my *MABQ* colleague who we met earlier. He would probably say something like, "Kilimanjaro sounds shit and cold.")

However, soon after that spark from our conquer zone lights up, a heavy, suffocating comfort blanket turns up to extinguish it. The rational, logical mind starts to say things like, "But you're already buying a new TV this year, and that Netflix subscription isn't free, you know. Can you really afford it?" or "Could you really take that much time off work?"

Before we know what has happened, our comfort zones have led us away from the exciting, impulsive, thrilling option and persuaded us to choose the safe path. And we feel satisfied, get a little dopamine rush and give ourselves a pat on the back because we made a 'sensible decision'. We have saved ourselves from wasting any money on such a stupid thing as a life-changing, soul-nourishing, inspirational adventure. Phew.

Kahneman realised this happened because we react differently to losing something real (e.g. money) than gaining something conceptual (e.g. the prospect of an amazing adventure). This is more commonly known as *loss aversion*.[27] Like so many of our instincts, it is linked to our evolutionary past. When faced with a decision, our primate ancestors would always, first and foremost, try to preserve what they had. It's the basics of evolution. If we saw a tasty piece of meat in the distance, but it was being guarded by a sabre-toothed

---

27   Kahneman, D., & Tversky, A. (1979). Prospect theory: An analysis of decision under risk. *Econometrica*, 47, 263-291

tiger, the caveman who focused on what they would gain (i.e. a meal) tended to be removed from the gene pool faster than a toddler who has done a poo in your local swimming pool. The more intelligent members of the tribe – most probably the cavewomen – who focused on what they might lose (i.e. their lives) were more likely to stay alive long enough to produce offspring who they would also teach about the pitfalls of playing tug o' war with a wild creature.

Fast forward 10,000 generations and we are presented with a world of highly intelligent humans who have a natural instinct for avoiding loss and staying in a zone of comfort – even if it means saying no to some things that are incredibly appealing at first glance.

The bad news, however, is that I can't undo the thousands of years of evolutionary psychology that is happening inside your brain (although I'm sure there is a self-help guru in California who can – for a fee). After all, no matter how hard I tried, when I decided to break a world record and fuck up my feet, 99% of my thoughts were my comfort zone telling me what a stupid idea it was. The next time you are tempted to step out of your comfort zone in any way, your brain will react in the same manner. But, then again, you will have the 1% – just as I did – that will be your conquer zone telling you to undertake that challenge. If you can design your environment and organise your thoughts in the right way, you might just be able to let your conquer zone be heard. And if you can do that, you can do anything.

"WE'RE GONNA NEED A BIGGER BOAT"[28]

"If someone offers you an amazing opportunity but you are not sure you can do it, say yes – then learn how to do it later!"

Sir Richard Branson

---

28   Spielberg, S. (director) (1975). *Jaws*. [Motion picture]

Sir Richard knows it. You know it. We all know it. But – as we've just seen – when faced with two options, our comfort zones always want to steer us towards the well-known, safer option rather than something more challenging but, ultimately, with more potential upsides.

Is there another way? There must be. If there wasn't, then we wouldn't have a decision to make. However, the fact that we are faced with a choice means the conflict between comfort and conquer is taking place within our minds. But how can we make better decisions? When choosing the more difficult path, I have always gained much more reward, and when I sat down and thought about it, I realised there was a strategy to give my conquer zone the hearing it deserved.

How many times have you been left floundering in a sea of indecision, struggling as giant waves of ideas, risks and possibilities are crashing down on you, plunging you deeper and deeper beneath the surface?

It's not supposed to be like this, and often it isn't. Most days, our comfort zones take all the hard work out of our decisions, and it feels like we are sailing calm seas on a luxury yacht: we are able to relax and drift quietly through life without really thinking or having a care in the world. Life is good. Life is comfortable.

Unfortunately, flat seas don't last forever, and a storm starts to grow every once in a while. The clouds can gather, and the disturbance can build without us realising it, and we don't understand that we are in the middle of a decision-driven depression until it is on top of us. Alternatively, we can be hit by a rogue wave out of the blue, and find ourselves capsized and failing in the water. On some occasions, we just decide to jump from the comfort of the boat into the sea, but once we hit the water we are unsure whether we will sink or find the strength to swim.

We've already seen how too many choices – or being faced with an overwhelming array of decisions to make – can cause our brains to shut down. This is because our comfort zones can't handle too much upheaval at once and start to hammer on our skulls to ask us to turn the volume down on our lives. After all, keeping our conquer zones quiet and restrained takes a lot of brainpower.

There is no way to avoid it, we *need* to make decisions. What's more, to fulfil the lives we dream of and embrace our conquer zones, we are going to have to decide to step towards short-term discomfort.

So how do we do it? Whether it's work, relationships, travels, adventures or challenges, we've all been faced with a dilemma whereby we find ourselves awake at 2am, unable to decide between the 'safe' option of the boat or the alluring unknown of the deep, blue water. The next day, we spill our hearts to friends and colleagues (most likely in a Starbucks, after standing like a zombie in front of the menu for 10 minutes), but we are still unable to make a decision. In despair, we then ask more and more people for their opinions on our dilemma, hoping desperately that someone – anyone – says the magic word or phrase that will make everything fall into place. The pain caused by a big decision overshadows everything we do because our comfort zones don't like it. But instead of trying to look deeper internally, we take this mental burden as a sign we need to search externally by discussing our dilemma with others.

Now, I'm not for a second suggesting that we should internalise our worries and struggles. One of the main causes behind me contemplating exiting a building from the roof rather than the ground floor was that I didn't share my dark thoughts and crippling self-doubt with others. When I did talk to some close family members and a few professionals with impressively framed certificates on the walls of their studies, I found it gave me immense relief and strength as I started the long, painful journey back to loving the person I saw in the mirror. For the avoidance of doubt: if any kind is shit it getting you down, *talk to someone!*

Nevertheless, when it's not a crisis but a decision we need to make, talking to a wide array of people might not always be the best option. It has the same impact as watching a YouTube video and expecting your life to change automatically. It won't. For example, have you ever had this kind of conversation with a friend?

Friend: "I just don't know what to do about this relationship/job/ adventure I've been offered."

You: "Would you enjoy it if you did it?"

Friend: "Yes, I think I would."

You: "Then you should do it."

Friend: "But what about my comfort/routine/current job/ lifestyle?"

You: "If you think it will make you happier, then you should do it."

Friend: "Yeah, but I just don't know. Maybe I'll ask someone else to see that they think."

It seems strange when we read these words on a page, but these types of conversations are happening every day. A person knows they have a decision to make, seeks the advice of others, gets even more confused, then searches out even more advice. It's like that person is drowning in a sea of uncertainty and calls for help, but then when someone dives in to aid them, they end up getting pushed beneath the waves by the very individual who they were trying to save. Nothing is achieved. The person with the dilemma is no closer to finding a solution, and the helpful friend ends up feeling like they would have been better-off staying high and dry on deck.

When this roleplay takes place, it's no one's fault. The person with the dilemma is genuinely seeking the counsel of others to aid them in making a decision, and the helpful friend earnestly wants to be, well, a helpful friend. Until the conversation happens again. And again. And again. You can only dive in so many times to save someone before you suggest they learn how to swim.

The helpful friend will tend to offer advice such as, "Have you tried drawing up a list of pros and cons to help you make the decision?" This is great in theory, but does little in practice to help solve the deeper conflict taking place between our comfort and conquer zones. When I couldn't decide whether to take the plunge and attempt to break a world record, my list of pros and cons looked something like this:

Attempting to become the fastest fisherman on the planet	
Pros	Cons
· I'll show some local children that they could achieve anything they set their little hearts on doing. · I'll get a nice certificate to hang in the downstairs toilet. · I'll forever have something to say when the dreaded 'tell us something interesting about yourself' question arises.	· It's fucking ridiculous. · It's going to hurt. A lot. · You might fail. · You will look stupid. · You might get heatstroke. · Your feet will get really messed up.

As you can see, the trusty pros-and-cons list is not perfect, and it is most definitely fallible. Even though I could see in black and white that attempting this challenge had way more disadvantages than benefits, and even despite the fact that some of these disadvantages weren't exactly small and inconsequential, I still went ahead with it.

Talking to anyone who will listen, writing lists, flipping a coin, and waiting an eternity for a so-called 'sign' all serve the same purpose. They pacify us and make us feel better because it seems as though we are acting towards our goals. Except we are not. These activities are just our comfort zones' trick to keep us in a bubble and prevent us from trying something, all while thinking we are doing something about it. Sneaky.

But all is not lost. There are practical, easy steps we can take to make decisions quicker. Unlike the 377 million (yes, this is a real figure) articles on Google that promise to help you make *easier* decisions, I can't promise these tips will help you make the best decision or the most straightforward or the least disruptive. But they might just help you make the *right* decision:

Give yourself a break: Remember all those self-help gurus who were telling you to break free from your comfort zone? When it comes to making a decision, they are wrong. Several studies have shown that, in order to get better at making decisions, we need to be calm, restful and focused.[29] It may sound counterproductive, but in order to decide whether or not to do something that will take us out of our comfort zones we need to be *in* our comfort zones to create the right conditions to think clearly.

A recent academic study demonstrates that just 15 minutes of meditation – mindfulness in particular – can help people with decision-making.[30] A series of experiments found that mindfulness meditation helped people to dampen the comfort-zone impulses buried deep in their brains. By taking the time to really consider the decisions they faced and the actions they could take, people could allow their comfort and conquer zones an equal hearing.

Rather than just reacting out of instinct and opting for the easy – or less scary – option, mindfulness allows people to review the information in front of them rationally at that particular moment. This leads to a more balanced discussion between head and heart, comfort and conquer. In turn, this enables people to understand what they really want and to go for it, rather than automatically making what seems to be the 'right' choice.

So, the next time you need to decide whether to take the adventurous path, risk doing something different, accept a challenge or try to break a world record, stop and take a breath. Consider where you are, what you want to do and how you can do it. In a world of a million crowded thoughts, try not to think at all. Instead, focus on feeling. And then go with what feels right.

---

29   A good place to start is: Soon, C. S., Brass, M., Heinze, H.-J., & Haynes, J.-D. (2008). Unconscious determinants of free decisions in the human brain. *Nature Neuroscience*, 11(5), 543–545

30   Hafenbrack, A.C., Kinias, Z. & Barsade, S.G. (2013). *Debiasing the Mind Through Meditation: Mindfulness and the Sunk-Cost Bias.*

Understand your goals: Do you really want to do this? If so, why? We are told two different stories every day. Our comfort zone has one narrative, which is designed to keep us cosy and secure. This story is focused on keeping everything we have presently. It is a story of preservation. Our conquer zone, however, is trying to tell us a tale of hopes and dreams. It is focused on the things we could achieve and become. It is a story of possibility.

However well-meaning our comfort zone is, and no matter how successful it is at keeping us safe and preventing us from losing too much time, money or effort, it is also very good at deceiving us. It can lead us to create goals that we *think* we want; in fact, we can be so convinced we want to achieve these particular goals that we will look our loved ones in the eye and swear this is something we desire. The truth is, deep down in our souls, we want something totally different.

Let's say you're offered an international assignment at work. Your boss sits you down and explains the situation: a new country, a different culture, more responsibility and reading the kids bedtime stories via Facetime for the foreseeable future.

You discuss the dilemma with your family, friends and anyone who you manage to corner who might be able to help you make the decision. "It's a challenge," you say. "It will be tough, but it could lead to that promotion and the corner office I've had my eye on for the last year."

On the surface, it seems a fairly simple dilemma: *Do I stay in my comfort zone or take the plunge?* But when you were so preoccupied with the deciding between never gaining access to the executives' bathroom or your children no longer recognising you, did you stop to consider what your goals really are?

I'm not talking about short-term goals such as the next promotion, the next pay rise, the car upgrade or those Jimmy Choos you've had your eye on for a month. I mean life goals. Where do you want to be next year, in the next five years or the next decade? When you're lying on your deathbed with your family around you, will you want to be happy that you chose to take yourself out of your comfort zone, but also your family zone and friendship zone? Or will you wish you had turned down the opportunity and focused your energy on that surfboard business you had really wanted to create since you were seven years old?

Professor David Welch at the University of Waterloo in Ontario argues, "People who aren't self-reflective are going to end up making bad decisions because they don't really know what they want in the first place."[31]

Deciding to leave your comfort zone doesn't mean that you're automatically entering your conquer zone. Without taking the time to really craft and hone your goals, and truly listen to and absorb what you want your life to be about, you could just leave your comfort zone and experience all that discomfort – all for nothing.

Taking control: Once you have made the decision, own it. So many times, we have decided to do something bold and scary and regretted it instantly.

When I announced I intended to become the world's fastest fisherman, my bold, decisive statement was met with laughter. However, the same people who found my idea so ludicrous had no problem wasting hours and hours of their lives talking about the things they would *like* to do if they didn't have so many excuses.

Don't dine out on dreams: I've witnessed people dominate a conversation for hours, prattling on about some big, bold challenge they are going to undertake. Their comfort zones have been putting them in this position for so long that they have got their pitch down to a fine art. You get the facts and figures; followed by how scary, dangerous and unique this adventure is; and then the long list of reasons why they won't be doing it up until some vague point in the future.

To go into your conquer zone, you don't have to tell the world

---

31   Welch, D. (2001). *Decisions, Decisions: The art of effective decision-making.*

about it, you just have to do it. A 50-year-old woman who quietly goes about fulfilling a lifelong dream to perform on stage is always closer to her conquer zone than a brash, 20-something guy who has spent the last year boring the pants off everyone by talking about the Bali trip he might take one day.

Another favourite game for a few so-called 'friends' (and Mr *MABQ*) was to dream up even crazier activities for me to try.

"Tell you what you need to do next, Freddie, try to swim around the world," one would laugh.

"Yeah, and after that you should try to climb Everest… in your underwear," added another with a chuckle.

There is a difference between acting like a dancing monkey just to try to impress some dickhead friends and actually deciding to do something you've always dreamed of and taking the plunge. It's about dreams, not dares.

You're not going on this conquer zone journey for the boasts, the accolades or the likes. This is about achieving all the things you've wanted to do but, for some reason, haven't given yourself permission to do so. It's not about proving you're the bravest or the boldest or the craziest. If people are impressed when you tell them what you've decided to do, then that's great. If they laugh and scorn, then they can go fuck themselves.

The most important thing is deciding what you want to do, and then taking control of your comfort zone, taking action and starting to get it done.

This is about you because it's your life and no one else's. Not your partner's, your kids', your dickhead friends' or your bosses'.

When it comes to the end of your days, it will be you giving your final breath, and it will be you deciding whether you have any regrets or not.

Because, as we're about to learn, we never know what is around the corner, and most of us have no idea how much time we have left to make our dreams come true.

FIVE

LOST TIME IS NEVER FOUND

"Your time is limited, so don't waste it living someone else's life."

Steve Jobs

It's Friday, 13th September 2019. I sit here in my tiny study, surrounded by pictures of my family, with reminders of my achievements and my medal collection on the wall behind me. The gleaming discs watch over me like an angel on my shoulder, reminding me that I can do anything I dream of, no matter how insignificant or useless I feel. They also sit behind me to represent these achievements happening in the past, a prompt to not dwell upon past victories for too long. They represent my comfort zone: something reassuring to have nearby but not to be my focus and not to be wallowed in. Ahead sits a window, with the sun of an unseasonably warm day setting behind trees and the roofs of tiny houses, the structures cutting large chunks of shadow out of the golden rays of light.

It's just after 8.30pm, and I should be settling into one of the finest delights my comfort zone has to offer – the Friday feeling. No matter where you are in the world, when the sun starts to dip on Fri-yay, you can guarantee that neckties will be loosened, drinks will be poured, sofas sunk into, glasses clicked, junk food ordered and almost every human will be breathing a collective sigh of relief. Another working week completed.

But, for me, it's not Fri-play at all. I'm sitting here, barely able to move within the suffocating grasp of anxiety, my eyes staring forwards, and still as stone aside from my fingers prodding at this keyboard in the same way a toddler shoves a hand into a cake before deciding whether to eat it. Without really knowing why it happened or how the strange combination of circumstances led me to this moment, I've realised I've stepped out of my comfort zone and into the wild, wide unknown. With small mouths to feed, a mortgage to pay and red bill reminders falling through the letterbox like clockwork, I have just quit my well-paid and awfully comfortable job.

How long was I in this illustrious role you ask? For how many years did I climb this particular corporate ladder, ascending carefully and monotonously, rung by rung, and accumulating knowledge and wealth every step along the way?

Four days.

Four bloody days. I started this job on Monday, and now it's Friday. I might have broken the world record for the fastest ever corporate career, and I didn't even have to wear a sodding fisherman's outfit.

Oh well, I tell myself, *it's only a job.* There are more important things in life. Like family, and health. And my wife has a job, so if needed, she can support us for a time while I look after the kids and keep on top of the housework. *No problem. Think positive.*

And then the panic attack hits, and my world turns to darkness.

Happy Friday 13th.

THERE'S NO PRESENT LIKE THE TIME

I've already mentioned that making decisions is easy. Even making a decision and then deciding again and again – no matter how much pain and anguish we face, and despite our comfort zones screaming at us to get back over here – to stay in our conquer zones isn't that hard.

But then life has a way of throwing curveballs to make us realise that time is running out.

Although the concept of 'not having enough time' is a myth, time itself is not. Time is slipping away like sand through our fingers, and nothing on earth can stop it. Sitting there on that Friday 13th, I was reeling from the decision I had just made. Quitting your job at any time is no small decision, but after *four days...* What the hell was I thinking? Just when I was reeling from this outcome, like a fighter on the ropes after receiving an uppercut, my panic attack turned up and dropped a nuclear bomb on the boxing ring.

What followed was a vicious cocktail of tears, shock, anger and a grave sense of injustice. *How could this be happening to us? Why me? Why now?* I was confused and afraid. Apart from the fear coursing through my veins like toxic waste leaking into the tributaries of a river, one emotion outshone all the rest: guilt.

I had decided previously that I was no longer happy in my professional comfort zone. I hadn't been satisfied in my career for a long time; for years and years, I had tried to be someone I wasn't. With the long hours, the networking drinks, the days and weeks away from my family, the expensive suits, the client drinks, the luxury hotels and the team drinks, I'd become someone I no longer recognised. The person I saw in the mirror was unhappy, out of control, unfulfilled and a shadow of the person I knew they could be. I was searching for something, but I didn't know what. In an attempt to find it, I had made the decision to leave my job and, potentially, turn my family's life upside down.

I'd always assumed that we had all the time in the world, but within the space of a few hours, it felt like time was abandoning me.

TIME BANDITS

Where did the time go?

Have you ever wondered if time is passing by too quickly? As soon as the summer suitcases have been put away and the kids have been packed off to school, we find ourselves saying something like, "Ooh, I can't believe Christmas has come round again already." The kids, on the other hand, are moaning that, "Christmas is aaaaaaages away," while eagerly watching the shelf every day, waiting for that bloody elf to magically appear on it.

Time is priceless because it is the one thing we cannot buy. No matter our background, income or job title, it is impossible to buy more of it or stop it from running out. Sure, we can eat a little better, drink a little less and decide to commit to a gym membership instead of a heroin habit. These things will probably extend our lives (unless your name is Keith Richards), but, at the end of the day, when our time's up, it's up.

How many times have we entered a job, relationship or unhealthy habit and told ourselves, *This won't be forever*? Then, before we know it, three years have passed, and we are still stuck there. We don't exactly hate our lives, but we also feel as if time has passed in a blur, and we're not quite sure how the hell we are still stuck in this situation, doing the same things, making the same excuses and having the same regrets.

But why does time fly, and what can we do to make the most of it?

Don't fear you have early-onset Alzheimer's. It is a proven fact that time does feel like it's passing faster and faster as we get older.

Firstly, it's pure maths. Let's take one year as an example and live those 365 days through the eyes of a five-year-old, a 40-year-old and an 80-year-old.

A year is 20% of a five-year-old's life.

A year is 2.5% of a 40-year-old's life.

A year is 1.25% of an 80-year-old's life.

It's the same unit of time, but it feels different depending on how many years have already passed us by. Imagine someone telling you had to wait 20% of your lifetime until next Christmas: no wonder kids are trying desperately to climb the chimney, looking for Santa's fat, red arse as soon as the Halloween costumes have been thrown in the back of the wardrobe.

There's a second, more scientific explanation for time speeding past us: it's all in our heads. The psychologist and journalist, Claudia Hammond, argues that it's because we assess time constantly in two ways. We look at it *prospectively*, in the present ("This journey is going really fast, isn't it?"), and *retrospectively*, in the past ("Didn't that holiday fly by?").[32]

When these two different perspectives match up, then time feels like it is passing at normal speed: what is happening today takes place at the same speed as what happened yesterday. Everybody's happy.

But when things start to get unbalanced, like watching the same movie on two TVs, one at normal speed and the other on fast forward, time starts to move more rapidly. Days feel like they are moving at normal speed, but the past turns into a rapidly spinning blur. The reason for this lies, unsurprisingly, in our comfort zones.

When we move into middle-age – the point in our lives when our comfort zones really start to dig their claws in – we tend to shy away from new experiences. The good old excuses start to come out: "I'm too old", "I'm too busy at work", "I've become too unfit", "I need spend time with the kids", or "My type 2 diabetes is out of control". Or maybe we are honest with ourselves and admit that life is just too damn comfortable, so why change things?

This makes us more risk adverse, more settled, more sensible and unlikely to try out new experiences. With the same old things happening day in, day out – the same commutes, same jobs, same people, same conversations and same meals – our brains find it more difficult to lock on to a reference point. The TV displaying time prospectively – today – is playing at normal speed, but the monitor showing time retrospectively – days gone by – is speeding up. We

---

32   Hammond, C. (2013). *Time Warped: Unlocking the mysteries of time perception.*

saw a great example of this during the 2020 COVID-19 lockdown. Because every day was so similar, they all started to merge into one, and we found it more and more difficult to keep track of where the weeks and months had gone.

Part of the reason for this time warp is that, as we get older, life inevitably brings fewer fresh experiences and more of the same old routines. Because we use the number of new memories we form to gauge how much time has passed, an average week that doesn't involve anything memorable happening gives the illusion that time is shrinking.

We often of talk of time 'passing in a blur'. We assume this refers to *velocity* because time feels like it is speeding past us. But there is also a second meaning: our memories appear blurry and unclear because all the days merge into one. Without anything different or exciting happening, the days of our lives all congeal into an unidentifiable, beige mush with fewer and fewer reference points to separate the memorable moments.

I know; appealing, isn't it?

This isn't exactly cutting-edge neuroscience. In fact, our conquer zones tend to sound the alarm and attempt to shake us out of his nondescript, blurry stupor sometime between the ages of 40 and 55. There is another name for this phenomenon: the midlife crisis.

But this doesn't have to be taken as a negative. By recognising that time is going to speed by faster and faster, like a snowball launched from the top of a hill, we can take action.

It has often been said that we overestimate how much we can achieve in a year, but underestimate what we can achieve in a decade. Time is like a new puppy: you can learn to direct its energy and let it help you create a more fulfilling, joyful life, or you can let it go out of control and shit on your carpet.

In the same way we underestimate how much attention a puppy needs, we fail to consider the impact time has upon our lives. Our comfort zones are amazing at surrounding us in a bubble called 'the holiday effect'. We've all been there, sitting in the sun lounger by the pool, enjoying the all-inclusive bar, and basking in the rays of sunshine that feel like they are recharging and warming the insides of our bones. We recline, relax, breathe that deep sigh and sip on the continental-strength Sex on the Beach cocktail, fully at peace and bathing in comfort. Then we blink and realise we've been sitting there for six hours. We're the colour of a cooked lobster, one of the kids has shit in the pool, and we try to stand up but fall over a collection of mostly empty plastic cocktail cups containing melted ice and browning chunks of pineapple. Our comfort zones have been so fulfilled that almost a whole day had passed us by and we didn't even realise it.

This tale may sound extreme (unless you have been on holiday with my mum), but it's just a high-speed version of what is happening in millions of lives every day. We get in a routine, we stay safe and comfortable, we do the same tasks, we speak to the same people, we drink in the same bars and we make the same mistakes. Our brains drift into autopilot, and even our comfort zones are sleeping at the wheel. Then, before we know it, another office Christmas party is upon us, and we wonder where all the time went.

Therefore, simply *deciding* to break the routine and go off-course is not enough. So many people decide to make changes to their lives, but then delay taking action. There is nothing malicious about it, and I'm not saying that taking time out for ourselves to rest our bodies and recharge our minds is a bad thing; in fact, it's quite the opposite. However, the trap we fall into is that we have the best of intentions, but time doesn't wait.

It is only when something happens out of the ordinary that we get a wake-up call. Like the drive home from work you make every single day, where you can't remember any detail of the journey until the day someone drives into your car at the traffic lights. Or the time you have just another repetitive day at work until your dad dies. Or the day the letter drops through the postbox confirming the date of your loved one's cancer scan.

It is a harsh truth of modern society that bad news tends to get our attention. We walk past miracles of life and nature every day without even raising our heads, but if we see a couple having a shouting match in the middle of the street, we stop and stare.

We've heard it so many times before: "Treat today like a gift, that's why it's called the *present*." Except we treat this present like it's a turd rolled in glitter that has been offered up by our worst enemy. The passing of time is the thing we fear the most, yet we take so little action. It's always 'tomorrow', 'next week', 'soon' and 'I should really get around to it'. And then it's not until life deals us a shitty hand that we realise it's too late.

I could fire motivational quotes at you all day, and tell you that life is short and you never know what's round the corner. I might get a reaction if I told you how quickly and easily life can be snuffed out in an instant, and death and tragedy could only be an hour or a day away. But I also don't want to waste your life with doom and gloom, and there are organisations such as insurance companies and political parties that do a much better job of running Project Fear than I could ever hope to.

How can I teach you something you already know? It's not rocket science. As far as we are aware, we have one life, and most of us just want to not fuck it up too badly. But there are things we can do to make the most of what time we have:

1. REALISE YOU'RE GOING TO DIE – AND THAT'S OK

We might as well start with a biggie. In Western society, we talk about 'escaping', 'cheating' or 'toying' with death. We think of the grave as something to be feared. It's the grim reaper walking around with a scythe, waiting to touch you with an icy finger, like the strange man who used to give all the children free ice creams in my local park.

But fear leads to inaction. If we fear something, then we put all our energy into staying as far from it as possible. Our comfort zones are designed to keep us safe and out of harm's way. This is why we take the easy route, the safe option and the well-trodden path, because a combination of evolution and societal norms has told our brains to work in a certain way. This – more often than not – keeps us safe. But even a Fort Knox-grade comfort zone can't protect us from death. In fact, never leaving our comfort zones is more likely to send us to an early grave because we will lack the variety that gives us stimulation and engagement. The phrase 'nothing to live for' was created for a reason.

When I stopped thinking of death as something to be feared, and accepted that it was a natural part of life, I realised it was easier to step into my conquer zone. I knew I was going to die one day and there wasn't a damn thing I could do about it, so I might as well try to chill out and enjoy my life.

Now I'm not saying you should be doing all kinds of stupid stuff and chasing down trouble as if you've got a death wish. After all, if you hang around the hair salon long enough, you're going to get a haircut. This isn't about taking risks in order to meet your maker sooner rather than later, it's about realising you're going to meet him (or her) one day, so you might as well enjoy yourself before that day comes.

Being OK with death isn't easy, but it is possible. Many different cultures accept death in a much more open and positive way than we tend to. In Bali, the *Ngaben* funeral ritual is performed to send the dead to the next life. During this custom, the family of the deceased treat the individual as if they are still alive. There is no mourning and no wails of grief are uttered because everyone believes that the deceased is only absent temporarily before being reincarnated. In Mexico, the *Dia de los Muertos* – the Day of the Dead – is a vibrant celebration of those who have passed away. Parties and parades are spirited and energetic, being loud enough to wake the dead and tell them they will never be forgotten.

These traditions exist not to celebrate or trivialise our mortality but to focus our minds on living in the present. We tend to fear death because we worry about what will happen to those we leave behind. But if we understand that our loved ones will think of us and smile when they remember the way in which we lived, it makes the concept of moving on a lot less terrifying.

We can write our own obituaries. We have the power to determine how we are remembered by others after we are gone. And the only way to create those memories is by deciding how we spend the time we have left.

2. YOU ALWAYS HAVE A CHOICE

Early on in my corporate career, when I was a fresh-faced graduate – young, dumb and full of, ahem, ambition – something happened, and even though I didn't realise it at the time, it was the beginning of the end. This event was monumental in its normality. It was so insignificant, so mundane, that it almost passed me by. But, somehow, the occurrence stuck in the dark recesses of my brain, and it was only years later I realised its significance. It wasn't a boardroom showdown, a shouting match across the office, punching my boss or turning up at the office with a hangover. It was my colleague Darren arriving at work one day.

Darren had the desk next to mine. A couple of years my senior, he would show me how to run a spreadsheet, attach a file to an email (yes, I know, this was pathetic, but it was 2005 and CD-ROMs were still bigger than Google, so this isn't *quite* as helpless as it sounds), take me to bars and then put me into a taxi hours later.

One Monday, Darren came into the office and slumped into the chair beside me. Blowing a huge sigh from his cheeks, like a deflating balloon, he cupped his chin in his hand as his fingers stabbed angrily at the keyboard in front of him, as if accusing it of some gross injustice. Not for the first time in my corporate career, I was confused.

Darren should not have been there. At that precise moment, he should have been sipping cocktails on a beach in Goa.

"Umm… Darren," I began to ask tentatively, almost certain I had got my dates mixed up, "aren't you supposed to be on holiday right now?"

"Yeah," he murmured, "I am, but a few things on this project needed my attention, so I cancelled the trip. You know how it is."

"Oh, of course," I responded, nodding eagerly like a puppy waiting for a stick to be thrown, while having absolutely no fucking idea *how it was.* "But… hadn't you been planning that trip for the last six months?"

"Yep, I guess so," he replied nonchalantly, "but that's the way it goes. I didn't have a choice. Mine's a double expresso, by the way."

While waiting in the queue at the coffee shop to collect my team's order (three years at university and £12,000 of debt had allowed me this responsibility), I couldn't get Darren's words out of my brain.

I didn't have a choice.

How could a fully fledged adult living in the civilised world feel as if they didn't have a choice? After all, he wasn't exactly in a North Korean gulag with a gun pointed at his head; he lived in central London and wore terrible Prada shoes.

But in the coming months and years after this moment, I found myself saying the same thing to others: "Sorry, I didn't have a choice." It became one of those reflex responses we give without thinking about it, with our comfort zones allowing our brains to take the shortcut and tell our mouths to utter the easiest response we can think of.

However, to step into our conquer zones and make the most of our lives, we must remember we *always* have a choice. We have a choice whether to do any of these:

- Keep going to that job we hate
- Keep returning to the partner we know isn't right for us
- Return to the same places and comforts again and again because they are familiar
- Turn down that challenge because we believe we lack the skills, confidence or time to complete it
- Put off doing something we *know* will make us healthier or happier in the long run because it is too painful or difficult in the short run

No matter how bleak or desolate our lives, we always have a *choice.* Even if you are in that North Korean gulag and big Kim is pointing a gun at you, you still have a choice whether to die crying or laughing.

3. FOCUS ON THE LITTLE THINGS, NOT THE BOLD GESTURES

I guarantee something will happen in your world – if it hasn't already, thanks COVID-19 – that will make you realise life is short. Maybe you or a loved one will have a cancer scare. Perhaps you'll have one of those 'if I'd left the house 30 seconds earlier, I'd be dead' brushes with fate. Or, possibly, you'll just look around at the beauty in the world and realise nothing lasts forever.

For me, as we know, it was nothing quite as poetic as this. I wasn't just hit with the uppercut of my dad's death but was also kicked in the balls by a colleague who'd decided to have a cardiac arrest in front of me a month later. 'Kicked in the balls' was a metaphor, by the way; my co-worker didn't literally pause his heart attack to punt me in the goolies.

Even though it feels strange to get a sudden reminder of our mortality, and we can feel oddly different to everyone else as a result of it, actually, it's perfectly normal. As any hard-nosed scientist will tell you: going through this experience wasn't fate, a sign or serendipity. The fact is that, by the time you've been around the block for 30–40 years, statistically, you're more likely than not to encounter at least one grisly, life-altering experience. Welcome to adulthood.

Statistics or not, this brush with death will most likely force us to look at our lives in a whole new light. We will want to transform our behaviours and help the world in brave and wonderful ways.

For a while.

Then, before you know it, you're back on the sofa, a slice of pizza in one hand and a warm beer in the other, and making excuses about all the things you'll do one day – as soon as you find the time or the money.

For most of us, this is natural. When my dad died and my colleague gave it his best shot, I was full of the 'grab life by the balls and shake it until it loves you' mindset (or something along those lines). By the time the funeral was over, I was a non-drinking, non-smoking, clean-living vegan who had paid a deposit to live in a Tibetan monastery for a month.

A week later, I was in the pub knocking back shots while shouting drunkenly down the phone to the credit card company that some hippy had stolen my identity and booked themselves a trip to the Far East.

Big life changes don't work. More often than not, the bolt from the blue or that moment of divine inspiration to make the most of our lives *doesn't happen*. We *think* it has happened, but we try to change too much, too quickly.

Like any natural, emotionally charged creature, our comfort zones go into shock when confronted with massive changes. For a while, it plays along because it can't quite believe what is happening. It's like when you're walking down Las Ramblas in Barcelona, and one of the street performers grabs you and insists you become the glamorous assistant for their show. You give one of those panicked, eyebrows-raised, *what-the-fuck-is-going-on* smiles, but, ultimately, you play along for a while. Your comfort zone does the same when you throw some massively unexpected behaviour at it.

Eventually, however, being the centre of attention for a street magician in a holiday destination gets unbearable and you walk away. The performer doesn't care as long as his mates had time to pickpocket everyone in the crowd. Your comfort zone is exactly the same: it plays along out of mild interest for a while, but then it says *enough is enough*. It wants to go back and get comfy by the pool.

Our comfort zones won't accept big changes. This is why it is so rare to wake up one morning and break those hard-wired, comfortable habits successfully. No matter what kind of wake-up call you get in life, if you're an overweight accountant from Rochdale named Derek, it's unlikely you'll wake up one morning and successfully become a bounty hunter in Belize or a spearfisherman in Indonesia. Sure, you'll make the *decision*, and you'll realise you want to have no regrets, but it's too much change too quickly. Your comfort zone won't be fooled that easily, and your conquer zone will still feel agonisingly out of reach.

A better approach is to make smaller changes. Rather than selling all your possessions to live a life of adventure as a circus performer, perhaps you could just decide to enrol in a local class to learn some skills. Then you could find a performance or show nearby to get to know some more complex routines. Next, maybe you could book a retreat somewhere sunny to experience the rigours of training and performing day after day. And, finally, you could spend a couple of weeks with a circus crew.

There are many different ways of realising your very own *The Greatest Showman* dream, but the aforementioned approach may result in more success than deciding to burn everything you own and rocking up on the doorstep of Cirque du Soleil one day shouting, "*Taa Daaah!*"

What I am absolutely *not* saying here is that you should abandon your dreams. If anyone is stuck in a rut and harbours a deep desire to do something different, challenging or a little bit crazy with their lives, then I will always cheer them on. We all have the potential and the abilities to step into our conquer zones and make our dreams come true. However, we can make that transition from *comfort* to *conquer* much more likely, easier and smoother by making small, measured, gradual steps, rather than taking a wild, flailing leap that – while looking pretty cool – might work but is also likely to be a spectacular failure.

4. DON'T WASTE YOUR TIME ON PEOPLE WHO DON'T DESERVE ANY OF IT

If you had £86,400, and someone stole £10, how would you feel?

- Would it ruin your day?
- Would it stop you from following your dreams?
- Would it make you change your appearance?
- Would it cause you to cry yourself to sleep?
- Would you still be replaying that moment in your head 10, 20, 30 or 50 years later?

Probably not. And if it did, then you really need to start this book from the beginning and get your priorities straight. Realistically, you would probably notice the loss, get annoyed for about 30 seconds, and then realise the bigger picture and get on with your day. You would focus on the shitload of good things you had going for you and not waste any more time on the insignificant thing you had lost.

However, we have 86,400 seconds in a day. An insult, cruel joke, badly spelled comment from a troll or just some poorly thought-out verbal diarrhoea from someone who didn't engage their brains before opening their mouths takes about 10 seconds of our time to register and process. But we don't accept it and let it wash over us like a breeze on a summer's day. We dwell on it, ponder it, let it consume us, repeat the harsh words back to ourselves and roll them around our mouths like a dodgy oyster we can't decide whether to spit back out or not.

So many times I was kept in my comfort zone because someone had told me I couldn't do something or wasn't good enough. On the occasions when I'd plucked up the courage to actually do something different from usual – and tried to take one step away from my fear and towards my goals – I'd hear the first negative comment and scuttle back under my comforting rock like the world's most sensitive crab.

When people take 10 seconds of our time to pay us a compliment, we tend to smile, make a bashful excuse and then move quickly on with our lives, not stopping to give it much consideration. But when we receive something negative or hurtful, we let it simmer and fester. Too much of our time is wasted on, to be frank, people giving us shit. We wouldn't go to these people for support or advice because we rarely value their opinions, so why give their abuse any more consideration?

A key aspect of making the most of our time is determining what we are prepared to tolerate. Work out how much shit you are prepared to take from people (here's a hint: none), and then draw your line in the sand. Anyone who crosses it should be ignored, and informed politely that they are overstepping the mark.

In the same way, once you have received that insult, don't waste any of your precious time getting drawn into a long conflict, argument or tit-for-tat mud-slinging. Why bring yourselves down to their level? It doesn't matter if they are a family member, partner or stranger in the street, remind yourself that if someone is insulting you, it's for one of three reasons: they are jealous of what you are doing, they are angry at themselves, or they are unhappy with their own lives. If you're really stepping out of your comfort zone, you might hit the jackpot and get all three.

Change always involves discomfort; you can hide in comfortable shadows and never upset anyone, or you can take the bold step forwards into the spotlight and accept some people will never like what they see.

5. DON'T BE YOUR OWN BIGGEST TIME-WASTER

It would be great if we could shut out the noise, though, wouldn't it? If we could just follow the aforementioned advice, put a middle finger up and shout, "*Fuck the haters!*" to the kind friend who only asked politely if you were going to be OK for money after you announced you were walking out of you job and booking a one-way ticket to Goa.

It would be easy if we were just to blame others for wasting our time and getting in the way of our goals. But we can't, because the biggest time-waster we face is *ourselves.*

Procrastination is the biggest killer of a dream. We already know that deciding to take that first step is so important, but after this point we have to keep the momentum. When we were teenagers and preparing for school exams, how many hours did we waste on 'getting ready' to revise instead of just cracking on with it? When the time came to hit the books, all of a sudden, I'd take it upon myself to tidy my room, organise my pencils, rearrange my desk, clean the hamster cage, have a snack and then have a poo – because I told myself that all these things needed to be done in order for me to plunge into learning. By total coincidence, all these tasks had taken me up to the time when *Baywatch* was about to start. And as every teenage boy knew, nothing got in the way of *Baywatch* time.

Fast forward a few years and not much has changed (but, sadly, nothing has replaced the image of David Hasselhoff running down the beach in slow motion). We decide to do something, but then immediately dream up a long list of things we need to do *first* in order to make it happen.

When it comes to setting aside our goals and ambitions for a rainy day, we can blame work, family commitments or a hectic social calendar all we like, but the truth is that nothing is wasting our time but ourselves and our own decisions.

You need to realise that if you have decided to commit to something that is important to you, then you must make time work in your favour. Your actions should be focused on getting closer to your goals, not throwing obstacles in your own path. After all, you've already made the brave decision to leave the comfortable path and take the more challenging, exciting route, but that doesn't mean you have to spend six months debating what shoes to wear before you can start the journey.

However, it is worth mentioning that there is a difference between 'wasting' time and 'resting' time. It's popular to talk about the hustle, the grind, the elbow grease and anything else that sounds like a title of a 1970s porno movie. I used to fall into the trap of thinking that relaxing, recovering and resting were a waste of my time. Then I got sick and injured because my body and mind were overworked and overstressed. Sure, this doesn't give you an excuse to pick up the takeaway menu and spend the next month in front of the TV, but never feel guilty about resting when your body tells you to. We need to sit back and gather ourselves before we can leap forwards.

*

Now we've learned how we can start to think about time differently. Hopefully, you are now starting to realise it's not about throwing yourself up the tallest mountains, running ultramarathons with a lion on your back, or thinking up the scariest, stupidest most challenging thing you can do just to impress people.

We all have different levels of comfort in our lives and different levels of desire regarding how far we'd like to step away from it. It doesn't matter whether you want to complete a race or sign up for that baking course you've always wanted to do. What matters is that you start to realise that your time is your own, you only have a limited amount of it, and you must use it wisely because you never know when it will run out.

But *why* is the concept of time so important when it comes to leaving our comfort zones? The next chapter will tell you, and I promise that you won't regret it.

SIX

NOTHING HURTS LIKE REGRET

"If you are not willing to risk the unusual, you will have to settle for the ordinary."

Jim Rohn

Why is time important? We can't stop it, we can't buy it, and we can't escape it. Why not just accept the inevitable truth that we have a finite amount of it and aim to spend it as wisely as possible?

The truth be told, that's not a bad plan. It's always advantageous to focus on the things we can control rather than waste precious time stressing about the stuff that is out of our hands. Whether it's moaning about a customer who is having a bad day, the traffic jam, the cancelled train or the creative toddler who decided to paint their latest masterpiece – on your new 4K TV screen – sometimes you just have to take a breath and accept shit happens.

But the passing of time is never smooth. Like a sports injury, it can keep us awake at night, it can strike us with pangs of pain when we rise in the morning, and it can buzz around our brains and distract us like a wasp at a picnic. However, it is not time itself that causes the nagging discomfort, it is the feeling we should have spent that time differently.

This sensation stalks us like a phantom in a haunted manor, making us feel as though we are trapped in a labyrinth from which there is no escape; it is a painful reminder of the choices we made or the decisions we failed to make in time.

THIS IS THE PAIN OF REGRET

There are two types of people in this world: those who say they have no regrets, and liars.

Many people say they have no regrets in life. They label themselves as carefree, immune to the burden of guilt or remorse, and appear to breeze through life on a whim with no regard to the what-ifs and the 'I wonder's. Bullshit. I have met with millionaires and people who live without a roof over their heads; I've encountered children who are embarking on the first tentative steps of their lives and elderly statesmen who have accepted they are taking their final lap on this earth; I've spoken to priests and prostitutes, judges and drug dealers, but no matter how different every person's life, they are united by one common feeling: regret.

I used to be one of those liars. I would fly through life with a *no-regrets attitude* (NRA). If you looked up this phrase in a dictionary, you would notice it has another meaning: 'acting like a dick'.

Like all the most dangerous habits, it crept up on me slowly, and I didn't realise I had a problem until it was too late. A selfish move here, a shrug of the shoulders there, and before I knew it I was struggling with a seriously dickish occurrence of NRA.

You probably know a fully fledged, card-carrying member of the NRA without realising it. However, like a watchful bystander at a sadomasochistic party, if you listen carefully for the right safewords, you'll be able to spot the main contenders quickly. And if you really pay attention, you'll notice there are two types of NRA members:

1. **YOLO warrior**: "It's all about living life to the full. Who wants to die with any regrets?" This type of NRA member is a smiling assassin. Initially, their words sound fine, aspirational even. But phrases like these are no more than a cloak for insecurities, hiding fear and cowardice behind a veil of excuses. The person who utters phrases such as these would like you to think they are always so far away from their comfort zone that they are teetering on the edge of adventure, like a sugar-crazed infant atop a flight of stairs. The truth is something different: they are selfish.

   While this individual would love to corner you at the office coffee machine and tell you how 'bonkers' they are, while pouring their beverage into a cup emblazoned with a slogan such as "You don't need to be crazy to work here, but it helps!" This *gung-ho* attitude masks arrogance and fear. You will soon discover that aiming to live life with no regrets equals thinking nothing of the feelings of others and not stopping to consider risks, consequences or the impact of their actions. They are a hormone-fed bull in an emotional china shop, destroying everything in their path in their pursuit of a 'crazy' life and making the most of their selfish, lonely time on this planet.

2. **The regretophobe**: "Hmm… I'm not really sure now is the time. I might regret it in the future." While the crazy YOLO loon in exhibit one is fuelled by misplaced bravado served with a side order of blind arrogance, this NRA member is powered by fear.

   Although they sit on the other end of the regret spectrum, they should be handled with equal caution. This person takes the meaning of 'no regrets' literally. They will do everything in their power to make sure they never regret a decision they make.

   They tell themselves the same old stories: be decisive, time is short and make the most of your life. These are lovely words if written on a piece of paper, but in real life are as practical as a condom made of Swiss cheese. There is only one way to regret nothing, and that is to *risk nothing*. A non-regretting NRA member (try saying that with a mouthful of Swiss cheese), tells themself a different but equally life-affirming story.

They *think* they are decisive, focused on adventure and pushing themselves to the limit, except they aren't. They are decisive, but only when it comes to choosing the safe, comfortable option. Like a 1950s racist boarding a bus in Alabama and choosing whether to sit in the front seats or the back, the decision is not even a decision. The faintest hint of actually doing something different from what they perceive as the norm does not even cross their minds. They are so stuck in their comfortable thought processes that they comfort themselves by thinking they are making a 'risky' decision, even when this is as far as possible from the truth.

Both of these characters have one thing in common: each of their comfort zones has assumed the driving seats of their brain, barricaded itself in and are fully entrenched in its position. Both the YOLO warrior and the regretophobe are powered by a desire to not waste the time they have in their lives, but in trying to do so, they cannot see they are in danger of squandering their potential.

I know this because I've been both of these people. I've used an excuse of "Who wants to have any regrets when they are older?" to justify my most foolish, idiotic actions. I used this line to excuse so much dumb shit: partying when I should have been working; buying crap I knew I couldn't afford; putting my own needs before others'; deciding to do any kind of activity I wanted to do when I knew there was something more important – but less fun – that I should be doing. I used that idiotic YOLO phrase to justify any kind of asshole behaviour that came into my brain.

At the other end of the spectrum, I used the fear of regret to stop me doing so many things I desperately wanted to do: moving jobs, making the most of opportunities, or changing cities, friendships or relationships. Any kind of potentially life-changing decision could easily be sidestepped by the convenient 'careful, you might regret it' get-out clause. All I had to do was remind myself about the risk of regret and, hey presto, I could stay safely in my comfort zone and not have to worry about improving my life. Before I realised the trap I had created for myself, regret had become more than an emotion: it had simultaneously become a catalyst for some seriously shitty behaviour and a harness preventing me from becoming the person I always wanted to be.

But what is regret? And – like a middle-aged, shiny-shirted, medallion-sporting lone wolf in a nightclub – once it has latched on to us, why is it so difficult escape?

REGRET-ME-NOT

Put simply, regret is the time we waste on wishing we hadn't done that stupid shit, and hoping and praying it can be undone. Alternatively, regret is the flurry of mental punches we batter ourselves with for *not* doing something, and wishing we could go back in time, *a la* Marty McFly, and make that decision again.

Regret attacks us with an onslaught of suffering, shame, doubt, self-loathing and disappointment. In many ways, it is not dissimilar to my own feelings when I used to open my school reports. And if regret has ever come knocking at your door, he probably didn't warn you he was bringing a plus-one: his close friend called *remorse*.

Although regret is generally regarded as the more popular of the pair – having occupied countless books, songs and films – it is actually the least impactful. We can feel regret for situations that don't affect us directly. If we see a news story about a natural disaster, for example, we can feel regret for the unfortunate souls caught up in the carnage, even if we know our actions – or inaction – has done nothing to cause it. (Yes, Greta Thunberg, I know our actions do contribute to climate change, but that's a story for another day.)

Remorse, however, is a shifty fellow. While regret is making you feel really shitty and taking all your attention, remorse is prising open the bathroom window and sneaking into your soul. Remorse is an emotion that is 100% caused by our own behaviour. Try as we might to blame others, the economy, the weather, or the fact we were tired, drunk, stressed or just plain couldn't be arsed, we know deep down that we are feeling remorse because we have done something (or not). And the fact we have no one to blame but ourselves makes us feel even lower. The dizzy, downward spiral of experiencing remorse, feeling shit, feeling more remorseful and feeling really shitty continues until the sensation haunts our every move.

While it would be tempting to devote a whole chapter to remorse, we're just going to show it the middle finger and keep moving on by. We tend to feel remorse when we've done something bad and we know it. This book isn't about stopping you from doing bad things (I'd suggest you look at things such as, well, laws to prevent you from doing that). We're here to live our best lives and make our dreams come true, which is a much more pleasant subject, so we'll continue on this cheery path of regret.

Regret is a negative mental state that we get ourselves into when we encounter a bad outcome, feel a sense of loss when we dwell on something that might have happened, or wish we could make things turn out differently. Regret is the trip of a lifetime we missed because we wanted that promotion, it's that partner we ignored our friends for who *did* turn out to be an asshole (hint: if your friends tell you he's an asshole, he's an asshole), it's the kisses that never happened, it's the opportunities that scared us too much, and it's the challenges that we assumed were beyond our capabilities.

Regret is the universe giving us a clip round the ear and yelling, *"Why didn't you just take the chance, you stupid fool?"*

But regret is important here because it is closely linked with *time*. How often have you felt regret and said something along the lines of, "I wish I could go back and do things differently," or "If I had that time again, I would have acted/said something/decided differently"?

Regret stalks us through time, not just because it reminds us of opportunities missed but also because it demonstrates that time is running out. Despite what the gurus tell us, the opportunities, decisions and crossroads we face throughout our lives are *not* unlimited; they are finite. And when we miss one, regret is the dark recesses of our minds telling us about it and warning us not to make the same mistake again – if we get the chance.

Regret also changes over time. Over a short timescale, people are more likely to feel regret about actions they *did* take. If in doubt, find a friend who decided to stay in the bar for that sixth tequila ("Because it's all about no regrets, right, guys?") and then woke up in their bosses' bed the next morning with a pile of sick in the corner of the room, and ask them what short-term regret feels like. As time moves on, however, and we get older and look back on our lives, regret will manifest itself in the things we *didn't* do. This concept was outlined by two professors of psychology, Thomas Gilovich and Shai Davidai.[33] But if the peer-reviewed research of two world-renowned academics isn't enough for you, why not call up that friend who will arrive on the doorstep with three bottles wine, ready to talk at you for the next two hours about why she should have asked for that guy's number back in 2008 or taken that job on the cruise ship 17 years ago.

Time can pour petrol on the fire of regret because it highlights and reminds us that some things are more difficult to change. As we saw previously, short-term regret is about *actions*, but if we react quickly, we can change something and make the regret go away. Feeling regretful about licking tequila off the bosses' stomach and the vomiting incident? A grovelling apology, some carpet cleaner, the world's biggest gift hamper or a long chat with HR will probably go somewhat towards reversing the regret, and you might even learn your lesson and do something different next time (I'm talking about a more holistic approach to team building, *not* swapping tequila for cocaine).

However, the long-term regrets are about *ourselves*. These run much deeper and are far more difficult to fix. You can talk to a therapist or a bartender about long-term regret, but there is a reason why psychotherapists drive Porsches and bartenders catch buses. The

---

33 Davidai, S., & Gilovich, T. (2018). The ideal road not taken: The self-discrepancies involved in people's most enduring regrets. Emotion, 18(3), 439–452

regrets about our lives involve our failures to live up to the dreams we had for ourselves, missed opportunities for love and the potentially life-changing decisions that we passed up.

Time may heal wounds, but if we're not careful, it can make the pain of introspective regret cut deeper. In 2009, Australian end-of-life care nurse Bronnie Ware wrote an article entitled 'Top five regrets of the dying', and three years later published a book of the same title.[34] She found herself in the unique position of being able to share the company of many terminally ill patients, and to listen as they contemplated their fast-approaching deaths and looked back on their lives. Unsurprisingly, none of the regrets expressed by the patients revolved around their bosses and shots of tequila, skipping that F45 class, or that 2am Netflix binge. When holding the hands of patients who knew they would soon be taking their last breaths, Bronnie learned the regrets of the dying involved not living the life they truly wanted, lacking the courage to express their true feelings and not giving themselves permission to be happier. Bronnie also stated, "All of the men I nursed deeply regretted spending so much of their lives on the treadmill of a work existence." Maybe drinking tequilas with the boss isn't such a bad idea after all: it could be a quick way to ensure you're not spending hours trapped in the job you hate. Any job. Ever again.

This is why time and regret are so intertwined. We so often fail to realise that our time on this planet is limited and ticking away relentlessly, and only when we receive a stark reminder – such as our own mortality – do we start to regret the things that really mattered. When staring death in the face, only then do we realise that we have become trapped in the same old patterns and habits that stopped us from doing what we really wanted. We became so addicted to familiarity that we vaguely wanted to change our lives, but never really had the drive, time or intention to take action. The one imposing, restricting trap that keeps us at risk of a life of regret is…

34 Ware, B. (2012). *The top five regrets of the dying: A life transformed by the dearly departing*. Carlsbad, Calif.: Hay House

Comfort.

And the sad truth is that we realise this all too late. What was common in the lives of the terminally ill patients is that they all had a deep, personal regret. They might have been successful, wealthy, and surrounded by loved ones and friends, but none of these things could prevent them experiencing some kind of regret that was now too late to change.

COMFORTABLY REGRETFUL

Now, I realise talking about dying and regret isn't exactly going to win any comedy awards. In fact, our normal instincts are to put these thoughts out of our minds and focus on something much more comfortable and pleasant. That's natural; after all, you should know by now that our brains are wired to seek pleasure and comfort, and to steer clear of morbid, mortal thoughts as if they are the passenger on the train who is talking to themself while licking the window.

It should come as no surprise that research shows the country in which people experience the widest-ranging and deepest feelings of regret is…

The United States of America.

That's right, people don't experience the highest levels of regret in war-torn, economically ruined or disaster-ravaged countries, but in one of the most powerful and prosperous countries in the world. That's not to say the US isn't without its problems, and its citizens don't experience hardships, but – on the overall comfort scale – it isn't exactly North Korea or Haiti.

Before I get the suits from the US embassy knocking at my door, I want to point out this isn't only the US's problem. Studies have shown that proportionally, regret is experienced more by people in richer, developed countries than in poorer, less-developed nations.[35] What's

---

35   For example, Roese, J. & Summerville, A. (2005). What We Regret Most… and Why. *Personality and Social Psychology Bulletin*. Sep; 31(9): 1273–1285.

more, in these richer nations, the middle- and upper-classes are more likely to experience regret than any other social demographic.

It is a quandary faced by people throughout the developed world: despite being enveloped in the comfortable trappings of an outwardly successful life – the house, the car, the ski holidays, the watch, the private schools and the enviable LinkedIn profile that has shiny-suited recruitment consultants 'reaching out' like participants at a bachelor party in a strip club – people are being weighed down by more regret than ever before.

Banking goliath Wells Fargo were kind enough to run a survey with almost 2,000 of its wealthiest clients.[36] Despite living a life of comfort that most of us could only dream of, almost all respondents stated they experienced deep regret on a regular basis. Around 15% of the investors said their top regret was not slowing their turbocharged ascent to the summit of the corporate world to enjoy life and savour experiences with loved ones. It was only when the wealthy clients reached the later years of their lives that they realised taking the time to rest, recover and enjoy themselves could have led in a healthier, happier existence.

Now, I'm aware that the super-rich believe they could teach us mere mortals so much about how to live our lives (usually this will involve us giving them money somewhere down the line), but we could also learn something from their experiences. The lesson they teach us is this: endlessly pursuing a gilded life of comfort does not lead to happiness, only to deeper regret.

I'm not saying this from my extremely cheap and regret-free high horse. When it came to money and regret, I was guiltier than most. For years, I pursued financial and career success at the expense of everything else, and regret crept up behind me and almost pushed me off a building. The times when I was at my happiest materialistically – when I was surrounded by opulent comfort – was when I suffered the deepest, most soul-destroying regret.

There was one night when I felt my life could not be pulled out

---

36 Wells Fargo Affluent Investor Survey. (2015). https://www.businesswire.com/news/
    home/20150715005418/en/Wells-Fargo-Survey-Affluent-Investors-Feeling-Good-on-
    Financial-Health-Yet-More-than-Half-Worry-about-Losing-Money-in-the-Market

of an uncontrollable tailspin of self-destruction, alcohol abuse, self-loathing and despair. Depression covered me like a dark cloak as I sat on a Mayfair pavement with my head in my hands, an empty can of lager in the gutter and cigarette butts lying around me like empty shell-casings from a machine gun. Even though the early rays of the summer sunrise must have been streaking across the turquoise sky, it felt as though my world was nothing but pitch-black.

The night in question was when I had been celebrating my promotion to the higher levels of the corporate ladder, which was a goal I had been striving towards for the previous 18 months. In that time, I had sacrificed the first precious months of my son's life, time with my wife, my fitness and my friends. In my obsession for the status and bigger pay cheque that another promotion would bring, I got drunk with, kissed the arses of and was bullied by people who I did not like and who had no respect for me. And I loved it. I became a person I didn't recognise or like, and by seeking greater wealth and external validation I was stacking up regrets faster than debts in the late-night casinos I used to frequent as part of so-called 'networking events'.

We've all read the inspirational quotes. We know that *happiness is a journey not a destination*; that we should not waste our lives working to make others richer; that we should not trade playtime for email time; and that it's wrong to sacrifice precious, limited moments of love for our own pursuit of success. Yet we still do it. We know time is short, and we know death will reach us all, but we are not willing to pursue what we truly love and makes us happy. And, deep down, we are scared we'll regret it.

I've driven a beaten-up Ford Escort and a tiny, old Vauxhall Corsa, followed by a battered BMW with moss growing in the windowsills, but I've never cried more tears and felt more lost and alone than when I was driving my turbocharged Porsche.

My happiest moments have occurred while I've been wearing a grubby pair of shorts and a stained t-shirt, but I've lost count of the times I've had my head in my hands while wearing a £1,000 suit.

My greatest achievements and successes have all happened with a

£100 Casio watch on my wrist, but I've lost and wasted hundreds of hours of my life while wearing a £3,000 Breitling.

And on that night when I should have been celebrating an extra comma being added to my bank balance, at that moment when I had finally achieved my goal, I saw no other solution than ending my life. No matter how many superficial achievements I obtained, and no matter how excited I knew I was supposed to be about adding another padded layer of comfort to my life, the regrets were still outweighing everything else. I knew deep down that this was going to end in one of two ways: a stint in a cell (padded or otherwise) or death.

Thanks to putting my hand up and asking for help (and a lot of it), I brought my mind back from the darkness. With gentle, patient help from loved ones and professionals, I saw there was a reason to live. I understood that suicide was a permanent solution to a temporary problem. I started to breathe again and started to remember the point of living. I felt gratitude, positivity and peace. With a smile on my face and a spring in my step, I lived happily ever after.

Bullshit.

REALISING WHAT YOU'RE MISSING

Things did get better. For a while.

But, unfortunately, I also got better at hiding the pain and regret I was still experiencing. When you're suffering from the blackness and despair of depression, the bravest, hardest and most important thing to do is to ask for help.

Once you've got that help, and you've had the conversations, cried the tears, examined the negative thoughts and taken the medication, you'll *want* to be better; I know I certainly did. Nevertheless, deep down, I still knew something wasn't right.

For me, this was as hard – if not harder – than putting my hand up and saying, "The black dog is on my shoulder," in the first place. I knew people were worried about me. I was certain that everyone

– including my family, friends, colleagues, bosses, the people on the suicide helpline who were sick of my voice, and the street cleaners who wondered if they were going to have to scrape me off the pavement one day – wanted me to be better.

But I didn't feel better.

What frustrated me most was that I had assumed that, after months of therapy and medication, I would be 'fixed'. Like when you take your car into the garage when it's making that strange rattling noise. Find the problem, go pay an expert to fix it, and then drive merrily on your way and get on with your life. I wanted this, everyone did, but that rattling was still there. Sure, it was quieter and easier to ignore, and it allowed me to believe I could turn the stereo of my life up really loud so that the persistent noise was harder to hear. But it never went away.

Even though I didn't want to listen, despite how much I simply *hoped* it would one day disappear, I also knew I *needed* to hear it. When I plucked up the courage to listen – bravery still fuelled by alcohol, I hasten to add – I realised that persistent, annoying, never-ending noise was not depression, but regret. Regret of living an existence that wasn't true to myself.

I'd realised I didn't want to die, but I did want to end that version of my life.

Through an ounce of strength, powered by the faintest glimmer of hope, I knew I hadn't gone through all this pain and torment and suffering to just go back to being the 'old me'. Through support, love and compassion, I had pulled myself back from the edge of despair, but I didn't want to go back to the place I had come from.

I always wanted to go home, obviously. After all, I sleep terribly on park benches. But I didn't want to go back to my old life of monotony, routine and stifling comfort. That nagging, rattling sensation was my conquer zone trying to tell me that another life was possible. Just because I had lost my way, it didn't mean that I couldn't see my goals and dreams, and I still wanted them. More than ever.

After all, I hadn't come this far to only get this far.

However, despite feeling like I had been given a second chance at life, and despite having to go through the pain of a mental rebirth, I was still too scared to step out of my comfort zone and go after what I really wanted. My comfort zone had been shaken and rattled, like the time I put my granny on a rollercoaster, and pretty soon it didn't know which way was up.

Similar to that persistent elderly relative who refuses to fall off their perch, it was still holding on with the grim determination born out of years and years of resilience. My comfort zone was still winning, and by winning it was still holding me back from doing what I really wanted to do.

If anything, coming out of my black hole of depression had given my comfort zone a whole new list of excuses to fire at me: "*You've been through so much, so take it easy;*" "*You need to focus on your recovery;*" "*Don't do anything that might stress you out;*" "*Give yourself time;*" and "*Focus on completing small tasks.*" All this was true (and great advice if you need it).

By now, it should be clear that we need to decide to take whatever action is required in order to move our lives towards our conquer zones. In order to push through with this decision, we have to recognise that our time is limited, and we want to avoid the pain of regret in the future.

But although we have three forces – decisiveness, time and regret – now pushing us out of our comfort zones and towards our conquer zones, there is still one big, fat, padded roadblock standing in the path to our dreams. Imagine you're running home from school, dreaming about raiding the fridge, donning your comfy clothes and collapsing on the sofa. Then the local bully steps out of the shadows and blocks your path. This is bad enough if you're a child, but even worse if you're a teacher.

Even with victory so close, with possibilities, positivity and excitement running through your body, there is still *one thing* that can drag you backwards like the inescapable gravitational pull of a planet you no longer want to be an inhabitant of:

The fear of failure.

SEVEN

FAILURE TO LAUNCH

"Success is not final, failure is not fatal: it is the courage to continue that counts."

Winston Churchill

"Freddie, you've had a really tough year…"

I offered a mild, sideways smile in response, but, secretly, my heart was soaring. Maybe this conversation with HR wasn't going to be as bad as I'd feared. Perhaps I'd just imagined all the missed deadlines; the frustrated, furrowed brows of my bosses; and the sighs of exasperation from my colleagues.

The HR director was right: it *had* been a tough year. My dad had died five months earlier, and, a few weeks after, a colleague had been kind enough to have a cardiac arrest in front of me. I'd done my best to gather up my grief and pain and then stuff it in a box somewhere up in the attic of my brain where, hopefully, it would all get forgotten about. Sure, there had been times when the stress had spilled out in the form of an occasional missed deadline, alcohol-induced blackout, or lack of care and attention in my work. But that was natural, right? Surely everyone who goes through a tough time gets a bit of a get-out-of-jail-free card?

"…and this is going to be a really tough conversation."

Shit.

Nothing screams 'middle-class comfort zone' like corporate failure. It has all the signs and symptoms of real failure – the panic, the helplessness, the tears and the confusion. But, at the same time, you have the vague impression that, in the grand history of the universe, the event causing you to cry into your coconut latte as you hide in the corner of Starbucks really doesn't matter at all. And this somehow makes it even worse.

As I sat in stunned silence in that meeting room, with my hands placed either side of an untouched plastic cup of water, my fingers pressed flat on the desktop to prevent them from shaking visibly, my comfort zone fell apart in front of my eyes. As my performance lowlights were read out in a cold, professional manner disguised as compassion – imagine both Siri and Alexa turning up to give you a motivational speech – phrases I never thought I'd hear directed towards me struck like jabs from a boxer: "lack of attention to detail"; "failed to keep your superiors informed"; "poor time management"; "ran over budget"; and "lack of confidence".

Up until this point, I had been staring at the deep, lush and inoffensively blue carpet as my charge sheet had been read out to me. But upon hearing that final comment, "lack of confidence", my gaze sprang upwards. There's no better way to give someone confidence than by telling them they lack confidence.

After the various policies, options, gardening periods and packages had been read out to me, I was asked to go away and have a good think about my life. As I staggered out of the office into London's spring air, it felt like I was emerging from a nightclub into a terrifying new dawn full of challenges and dangers. On the bright side, I knew I had the ability and capacity to make some decisions about what would happen next. I also had a new sense of the importance of time (thanks, Dad). But what I also possessed was an extraordinary amount of fear, mixed with a huge sense of failure.

Failure is an ominous, sinking sensation that drags you down and entraps you in your own weaknesses. No matter how many times you read the motivational quotes such as "failure is the best thing to ever happen to us" or "the path to success is lined by failures", and no matter how often you watch the YouTube channels where millionaires preach they love failing *every single day*, nothing stops the deep, terrifying desolation.

When life exposes you, and then takes a run-up and kicks you right between the legs, no amount of positive thinking is going to stop the pain forcing you to your knees.

This is how I felt as my corporate career, which I had built up over the last 14 years, fell away in front of my eyes. No matter how much I tried to believe the words I was telling myself about it being *a learning opportunity, a chance to show them what I'm made of*, or *a great way to demonstrate I'm a key asset to the team* (I almost threw up a little in my mouth when I wrote that one), there was no denying that I felt as if I'd taken an absolute beating.

Now, like I said, when it comes to catastrophic failures that have befallen mankind, I realise this wasn't exactly up there with the designers of the Titanic when they signed off on the 'absolutely unsinkable' blueprints and then rushed off to the pub for a couple of pints, but it doesn't matter. Failures aren't comparable; they are relevant to every person's history and circumstances, and that is what makes them even more cripplingly painful: they are targeted at your weaknesses.

I didn't realise it at the time, but my job was my weaknesses. I needed that career for the stability and income it afforded me, and because it fuelled my ego. Take a kid who grew up in a household where no one had a stable career – where jobs, people and possessions came and went – and then add a shitload of financial insecurity on top of that. I'm no neuroscientist or psychologist, but I'd take a pretty good wager as to why, for me, nothing was more important than securing a stable, corporate job with the comforting cushion of a monthly pay cheque. But, despite this, I had known I was a fish out of water right from the beginning. On day one, while the rest of the trainees were setting objectives and key performance indicators, and networking with the new boss, I was marvelling at a magical machine that gave me as many free coffees as I wanted.

Consequently, my comfort zone was accustomed to telling me lies. It told me this was the career I wanted, that I was doing the things I wanted to do and that my dreams were coming true. In reality, this was bullshit. Because of my uncomfortable upbringing in terms of money and security, I had sought comfort in stability. Once I'd achieved that sensible, stable life, my comfort zone set up camp, and was moving for nothing and no one. It was like the parent who loves camping and drags their family across fields and over hills, and will happily sit in a wet tent, undercooking sausages, merrily ignoring the pleas and protests of their loved ones, who just want to go and do something they actually enjoy.

So, even though I knew this corporate life wasn't for me, I allowed myself to become trapped by my comfort zone. As the years went by, the pension plan stacked up, the bonuses got bigger (marginally), the car payments got larger, the house needed extending, the kids kept growing, and I got more and more entrenched. As my comfort zone literally grew around me, I became safer and safer in my decisions. At some point, my thinking shifted from doing what I *wanted* to doing what I *needed* in order to preserve my level of comfort. I became unwilling to do anything that carried the slightest hint of failure, lest it put my comfort zone in jeopardy.

I would openly discuss with friends and family how much I hated my career, but I couldn't see a way out. Or, to be precise, I could see plenty of escape routes, but all of them involved a bit of discomfort along the way. At that time, I was settling for a 6/10 life – and probably a 4/10 version of myself – all because I was obsessed with not losing what I had, which – in my eyes – would mean I was a failure. Who chooses *voluntarily* to step away from a certain standard of living and income? As far as I was concerned, if I did this, I would be failing my family, my kids and myself. I'd be big, fat Freddie the Failure. My comfort zone was not going to let this happen, so much so, in fact, that I even created a little mantra for myself: 'Freddie never fails'. Yep, I was *that* kind of corporate dick.

Failure is a close relative to *karma* in that it tends to find a way to bite you on the arse and teach you a lesson when you least expect it – but also when you need it the most.

In my career, I was so busy focusing on 'not failing' that I was neglecting so many other aspects of my life: my wife, kids, health and friendships. Most of it went down the toilet because I was focused on protecting the sacred fortress that was my job. And don't forget that this was the fortress I spent the previous couple of years bitching and moaning about. It's like when you go and visit your granny, and she complains about her carpet, loud neighbours, bad weather, steep stairs and broken TV ("The TV's not broken, Granny; you just put the remote in the microwave."). But when you suggest she moves, she looks at you like you just kicked her cat and exclaims, "*Move?* Why would I move? I love it here!"

Well, I know just how Granny feels, because I was the same. When anyone plucked up the courage to suggest gently that I left the career I hated, my comfort zone would spring into action. My favourite response would be, "If we want to have the nice car, the big kitchen, the posh restaurants, the ski trip, the summer holiday, the iPad and all the TV channels... then I need to go and do this thing I hate."

My comfort zone told me this amazing lie, and because I believed it, I repeated it to everyone who dared to ask me why I spent so long doing something I hated. And the real beauty of it was that *I believed it myself.* At that point in my life, I thought success and happiness came from doing the things we didn't want to do. After all, no one enjoys their job, do they? They all hate their careers, right? It's normal to sit in the toilets for an hour with your head in your hands, trying not to cry... isn't it?

At the precise moment when this particularly grubby and uninspiring carpet was being pulled from under me, all I could think about was clinging on for dear life. Anything else would be failure.

DRINKING FROM THE FAILURE FOUNTAIN

After I received what felt like the most devastating news of my life – that my career was being flushed down the toilet (and, yes, at the time that included the phone informing me about my dad's upcoming death – seriously, what the fuck?) – I found it impossible to see any positives. Standing outside my office, I was stunned and unable to process the information I'd just received. In many ways, the emotions I experienced mirrored those from when I stood outside the Royal United Hospital, trying to get my head around the fact I'd just watched my dad die: I was numb, knocked for six, and wanted a beer and a smoke.

The failure I'd feared the most had presented itself and poked me in the eye. As I sat in a pub, sipping a beer – to chase down the three drinks I'd sunk so quickly they hadn't touched the sides of my throat – I tried to console myself with every motivational YouTube video and inspirational article I could find. I googled every term you could think of: 'embracing failure', 'learning from failure', 'making friends with failure' and 'you shouldn't have failed, you stupid fucking failure'.

But no matter how hard I tried to motivate (or drink) myself out of my pit of despair, I couldn't see past the fact that I had messed up. Big time.

Now I wouldn't be the first person in the world to loathe the sense of failure. Many people have felt a lot shittier about messing up a lot worse than I did. As children, we are usually taught that failure is a part of the learning process: learning to walk involves plenty of falling down, learning to eat involves spoonfuls of mashed potato in the eye, and learning to use the toilet involves a lot of puddles. I say this is *usually* OK because there will always be the one mother or father who insists on their child being perfect from the day they were born, and then makes it their mission to rub this perfection in the face of every other parent, like a prison-yard dirty protest.

As babies and toddlers, we don't even think of failure as a concept. It is just something that happens as naturally as having a tantrum when a sandwich is cut into squares instead of triangles. From about the age of eight, we start to develop a sense of self, and we care about how other people perceive us. This is also around the time parents shift from being 'wonderful' to 'slightly embarrassing' in their children's eyes (years later, mums and dads will usually progress to become their child's 'worst fucking enemy'). It is at this age when we start to care about failure. We notice the people in our class who are passing the spelling tests and those who are stuck on C-A-T (that'll be me). We start to get upset when we're last to be picked for the team in PE (hello, me again), or when it comes to the festive show and the teacher informs us we've landed the prize role of a tree (hey, I brought *a lot* of depth to that role).

In recent years, society has done its best to cushion these failures for our children. We create a world of comfort, furnished with 10th place medals and a tremendous sense of superiority that our little darlings can do no wrong. But as we grow up, we often learn the hard way that we *do* mess up, screw up, fail to meet to the grade, or are simply really, naturally shit at some things. The deeper and more expansive the comfort zone we (or, to be precise, our parents) have created, the harder it hits when we inevitably encounter failure. When we fall, our comfort zones do not protect us. In fact, the greater the comfort we are used to, the more painful the landing when our world falls apart.

As teenagers and young adults, we cultivate a greater fear of failure. We don't want to look bad, mess up or do anything that generally risks ridicule. This is why adolescents prefer to stay in their bedroom, glued to their phones and typing away with an impossible blur of thumbs like the Flash is suffering from Parkinson's disease. Why do anything new and risk failure or embarrassment when you can live your life through the comfort of a screen?

But the interesting part happens when we become more mature adults. I say 'more mature' because, typically, Westernised young adults in their 20s are experiencing an extension of their comfort-filled childhood in which a complex support network of parents and friends prevent any major self-inflicted fuck-ups or failures. When I say 'support network', that's a polite way of saying that many parents are crossing their kid's palms with silver to ensure the little darlings never have to get their hands dirty. A recent survey by a soft and fluffy philanthropy institution, otherwise known as Merrill Lynch, showed that in 2018, 79% of parents with adult children provide some sort of support for their living expenses.[37] In fact, the research shows that parents are spending a combined $500 billion on their grown-up kids – double what they're putting towards their own retirement.

It not as simple as it seems, however. The story of 'parents providing an emotional and financial comfort zone for their pampered, millennial kids' isn't exactly groundbreaking (although many people appear to dine out repeating this tale). The conundrum appears when adults are bombarded with the message that it's OK to fail, while simultaneously putting the systems and controls in place to ensure that failure will never, ever happen to their children.

Looking back through history, failure was not embraced in the same way as it is today. When the Great Fire of London was finally extinguished on 6th September 1666, following a small but fairly significant screw-up in Thomas Farriner's bakery, there weren't any inspirational phrases daubed on walls saying things such as, "Failure sparks the blaze of success". No, our baker Tom had royally fucked up, and you can be sure he knew about it. Before he died, at least.

But, today, failure is not only accepted but encouraged. Do you happen to lead a financial institution responsible for a global financial economic crash? No problem! You are officially too big to fail! Were you found guilty and imprisoned for stock-market manipulation and defrauding thousands of people of their life savings in a penny-stock boiler-room scam? Congratulations! You are the proud subject of an Oscar-winning movie, write best-selling books and have a lucrative public speaking career![38]

Failure is now embraced like the prodigal son. It is welcomed,

---

37 Merrill Lynch. (2018). *Financial Journey of Modern Parenting, Including Joy, Complexity and Sacrifice.*

38 Belfort, J. (2007). *The Wolf of Wall Street.* Bantam Books.

encouraged and praised by billionaires and entrepreneurs alike. It is, we are told, the only way we can experience true success. And you know what? They are probably right.

So, why do we still fear it so much? And why, when failure smacked me across the face, did I cower and fall instead of jumping with triumph?

BE CAREFUL WHAT YOU WISH FOR

We all enjoy a good daydream. Standing in the shower, my head bowed as the water cascaded down my face, I had run through the scenario so many times in my head: *sitting in a meeting room with my boss, giving me an opportunity to be honest for once: a time for me to say the things I've really wanted to say and then walk out of there forever.*

In my mind's eye, it would be akin to one of the great Hollywood scenes from movies such as *American Beauty* or *Fight Club* where the harassed, depressed, unhappy worker finally builds up the courage to tell their boss where to shove that corporate job.

In the final, terminal meeting with my HR director, I had that moment. The open goal was in front of me and all I had to do was nudge the ball into the net.

And I missed.

That's the interesting thing about failure: failing at something kills us, even when we didn't really enjoy that particular activity in the first place.

But here's where it gets *really* interesting. Looking back, I realise I wasn't devastated by failing in my career at all. What destroyed me was the thought of losing all the things I associated with that job:

- The money
- The nods of approval from family members, clients and strangers when I mentioned the company I worked for

- The sharp suits and expensive watches
- The luxury holidays
- The first-class travel and five-star hotels

The trappings of the life I have just listed can be summed up in one phrase: comfort zone.

Even though I hated my career, it had allowed me to create a comfortable, bloated, expanding waistline of a life for myself. And now this existence was under threat. I was like a spoiled child with a playroom piled high with toys, who cried when someone tried to borrow a piece of plastic tat that I'd forgotten about long ago.

This is why so many of us (me included) fail to take action, even when we know what we really should do. How many times have we watched the gurus as they say, "Follow your dreams"; "Take the risk"; and "Life's too short". We roll our eyes, have a swig of our beer and say something along lines of, "Yeah, right… It's easy for them to say, but they've never had the hardship of the BMW payments, private tennis lessons, holidays at an exclusive resort, TAG Heuer watch and a cocaine habit to pay for. If I didn't have all these things hanging over me… then, yeah, maybe I would follow my dreams."

Our comfort zones were not something imposed upon us, such as an illness, physical ailment or natural disaster. They are our creation. We build our castles of comfort as high as our budgets allow. And, in most cases, those walls still aren't high enough, so we borrow money to create a seemingly impenetrable palace of comfort. Once we are established in this kingdom, we are prepared to defend it at all costs.

I'd been building my palace of comfort for years. When I wasn't building it, I was looking over at my friends and family to see how their own constructions were getting on. If I saw them creating castles that looked even more plush, luxurious and comfortable than mine, I'd get jealous. Instead of enjoying what I had built, I'd kick the walls and sigh at my 50 inch TV as I sulked at how much others had in comparison to me. Paying some attention to the people with much *less* comfort than me – or no comfort at all – didn't even cross my mind.

But then my castle of comfort faced its greatest threat yet. It was akin to a breathtaking siege scene from one of the films in *The Lord of the Rings* series, except a blood-thirsty army of marauding orcs was replaced by a HR director with an axe to grind and a headcount-reduction target to hit. And, like any respectable anti-hero, when I came under attack, I got angry. But then I panicked.

When our comfort zones come under attack, and when our patterns, traditions and ways of life are threatened, we react instinctively: fight, flight or freeze. Have you ever experienced those few seconds of sickness, that quick lurch in your stomach, or the rapid tingle as sweat caresses your palms when one of these happens:

- A letter from the taxman arrives
- A late, unexpected knock at the door is heard
- The credit card company phones
- Your boss asks if they can have a quick word

Our instinct is always to consider how much we have to lose. And that threatened feeling of panic – no matter how irrational it seems afterwards – is our comfort zone wrapping its arms around everything we have created and shouting, "*You can't have it!*"

When my career failure hit, it was like I'd been pushed into a darkened room. Everything seemed unknown, different and forbidding. It wasn't until later (*much* later) that things started to come into focus. Once I'd stopped panicking and letting my mind be filled with fear at the concept of a destroyed comfort zone, I started to see things in a different way. And two beacons of enlightenment shone through this new, terrifying darkness.

1. **I deserved it.** I don't mean this in a "woe is me; I don't deserve happiness" kind of way. We should never think we don't deserve great things to happen to us. But in this particular instance, maybe I did deserve to get my arse kicked.

    When the news hit me, I reacted with all the "*how dare they treat me like this?"* bluster of a golf club president who has found a children's ambulance in his reserved parking space. But once the dust had settled, and I sat in the ruins of my destroyed comfort zone, I was finally able to see my conquer zone in the distance. From that vantage point, I could also see myself and my actions from a new perspective.

It was time for some home truths. I'd been devastated when I'd been hit by corporate failure, but if I were totally honest with myself, I had it coming. I had – once upon a time – enjoyed my job. Yes, maybe I'd just told myself that lie, but it hadn't been a falsehood that I'd also been good at it. I'd received promotions, pay rises, standing ovations and glowing performance reviews, so I'd be lying if I said I'd been living in some kind of Dante's Inferno-type hell. But once my dad had died, my heart was no longer in the corporate world. Rightly or wrongly, I just didn't want my life to be about making other people a lot richer while making myself a bit richer and a lot more stressed in the process. And it showed.

I took my eye off the ball. Turning up at work at 8.30am started to merge into 8.45am, which morphed into 9.00am, which somehow got pushed to 9.15am and then 9.30am. Once I'd carefully planned my morning arrival to coincide with going for a long coffee and then a poo, I would suddenly find myself with only half an hour to go until lunchtime. Then, when the clock struck 4pm I would start telling myself stories such as, *"You don't want to regret missing time with your children while being stuck at the office,"* and would pack up my things to make a swift exit. Combine this with a general lack of attention to detail, letting the quality of my work slip, enjoying the free bar at 'networking drinks' a bit too freely, and everything pointed to one highly scientific, conclusion: I was being a dick, and a lazy one at that.

Anyone who has watched *The Apprentice* will know that acting like a dick in business is forgivable. In some industries it's actively rewarded. But being a lazy, selfish dick with poor attention to detail is a no-no.

I had fallen into a comfort trap of thinking that my corporate job existed purely to fund my increasingly lavish and hedonistic lifestyle. While guzzling hungrily at the corporate teat, I forgot that my company, colleagues and clients wanted and needed me to be a switched-on, high-performing and generally non-dickish human being in return.

It was only when my corporate comfort zone was destroyed and I was forced to step into my conquer zone that I could see the truth: *I deserved to fail.* It was as if I was so unhappy with my life that I had brazenly been daring my company to take action. My attitude was getting worse and worse, like a child in the airline seat behind you who starts kicking, poking and then throwing. Everyone's patience runs out eventually. Once outside my comfort zone, I transformed from being indignantly offended that they had dared to call me out on my poor behaviour to being impressed that my company had supported and carried me for so long, and only surprised they hadn't pulled the plug sooner.

This type of clarity is only something I found *after* I set foot in my conquer zone (and let's not sound too brave here – remember that the only reason I got into this particular career conquer zone in the first place was because I'd been fired out of my comfort zone in a cannon). But there was another beam of enlightenment coming my way as well…

2. **I could see clearly.** When the P45 hit my doormat with an ominous thud, the song 'I Can See Clearly Now' was playing on the radio. I sang along, but with different lyrics about the Porsche, Gucci trainers and weekend skiing in Davos that had gone.

Admittedly, it was not very catchy. That was the start and finish of my singer/songwriter career.

If you were paying attention earlier, you'll remember I realised it wasn't the actual failure of my job that was eating me up inside. It was the failure with respect to all the flashy material things that I associated with that role, and threat of not being able to afford the crap I would usually purchase to make myself feel better. But when I was able to take a step back and examine these thoughts with an ounce of time and perspective (and, let's face it, time and perspective were two resources I suddenly had in abundance), I was able to see them for what they really were. Let's take a look at the material things I was so terrified of losing, but with a conquer zone lens:

1. The *money* – OK, we need to get the big one out of the way first. There's no hippy-dancing around the forest singing 'All You Need Is Love' with this one. My corporate failure meant I wasn't going to be skipping along to the bank any time soon, and this was going to hurt. Like it or loathe it, money equalled options.

   But as we saw earlier in the book, money is a key comfort zone enabler, and although I suddenly had less of it, I didn't seem to notice. For example, my job paid well, but it didn't allow me to go and buy a Ferrari or anything, and that still hadn't changed. Plus, because I wasn't desperately unhappy every day, I found that my hedonistic spending went from budget-version *The Wolf of Wall Street* to zero.

   I'm never going to pretend that money isn't important to me. In fact, after growing up with such financial instability, I developed an unhealthy attachment to it. In the past, I would have done anything to keep it, or sacrificed anything to get more of it, and the concept of doing anything that would result in losing it was the most alien thing in the world.

   But now I had been forced from the money room like an ordinary reveller who has smuggled their way into Jay-Z's VIP area and just been ejected. When my arse landed on the pavement, I learned a few things about money:

   • *You don't need a lot to feel well-off.* I could still say yes to the coffees, the ice creams, the school trips and the zoo visits, I just had to say no to other things – like cocaine.

- You spend to meet your budget. When my monthly income was five times higher than it is now, I would just do more expensive, pointless, dumb shit to have fun. Now I have a different kind of fun that actually makes wonderful memories. I still get the same (if not better) emotional high, but it costs me a fraction of the price.
- I used it as a comfort blanket. I would literally wrap myself up in £20 notes if I could have, like wearing the world's shittiest but most expensive bulletproof jacket. If I knew I didn't have a certain amount of money in my savings account, I would suffer panic attacks, despite not having a cause nor a need for such a financial safety net; I just thought I needed more. Now I was forced to throw that comfort blanket aside, I felt like a stronger person.

Losing the thing that brought money into my life (i.e. my job) allowed me to release myself from my financial handcuffs. Instead of sleepwalking from pay cheque to pay cheque, I found I had to give myself a kick up the arse. I had to be resourceful, imaginative, disciplined, engaged and attentive, all to make what I had stretch further and somehow create more.

This certainly isn't one of those disillusioned 'Oh how fun and liberating it is to be poor!' comments the 1% make. Being poor sucks. I know that. We all know that. But what didn't suck was knowing I had to use my brain and my skills to get out of my comfort zone and provide for my family. If I could do that, maybe I'd no longer be quite the failure I saw myself to be.

2. *The nods of approval from family members, friends and strangers when I mentioned the company I worked for.* This one hurt me more than it should have. In the past, I loved to name-drop my employer into my conversations, only to receive a comforting chorus of oohs and ahs from whoever was unfortunate enough

to be in the vicinity. Even when I saw my company in the headlines for the wrong reasons, I'd boast arrogantly that I worked for them.

However, once I had my conquer-zone clarity, I realised something: I loved *telling* other people about that job a hell of a lot more than I actually loved *doing* it. And really, who actually gave a shit? When was the last time you were talking to someone at a party, learned about their trade or profession, and actually remembered and/or gave a shit even half an hour later? And even if you *did* happen to recall that one interesting person, I can guarantee they weren't selling their soul to be a management consultant like I was.

With the benefit of clarity, I realised suddenly that the most interesting people at parties were the people who were doing something different, forging their own paths and trying to make their unique imprint on the world.

And, most importantly, why the hell should I care about impressing strangers at parties? I didn't know them, certainly didn't love them, and therefore shouldn't be valuing or indulging their opinions in the first place. And, besides, I was always hammered at parties, because I was downing drinks in a poor attempt to cope with working the previous five days in that job I hated.

3. *The sharp suits, the expensive watches, the luxury holidays, the first-class travel and the five-star hotels.* Confession time. Now the comfort-tinted spectacles had been taken off, I could indeed see clearly, and foremost in my vision was that I had become one of *those* people. Yep, the people who do something like this:

- When meeting you, give you a microsecond look up and down to judge your outfit and estimate whether it was more expensive than theirs.

- Make a semi-sexual 'phwoar' noise when someone in the group (while clustered at a bar table full of drinks, no doubt), pulls up a shirt cuff to reveal a new watch.
- Moan about how impossible it is to find uncrowded ski slopes in Europe any more.
- Make a genuine, heart-felt complaint that staying in anything less than a four-star hotel was damaging for my mental health.

Oh yes, dear reader, I was a special kind of dick.

But the thing is that, deep down, I knew I wasn't a dick (although I'm sure you may beg to differ). Despite being brought up with little money, I was taught manners, kindness, decency, to help people and to give something back. Somewhere along the corporate journey, I had forgotten who this person was. I left them in the distance as I zoomed off for something more glamorous and more exciting, chasing the next bonus and share payout.

I became so consumed with earning and consuming that I forgot about giving, loving and living. But when I failed in my career, I was able to rediscover the person who I wanted to be once more. I realised that, while the material shit was pretty (and, let's face it, pretty fun), it didn't actually matter.

THE FUCK-IT BUTTON

I would love to tell you there was a grand strategy. It would be so inspirational to say I made the key decisions wisely; I realised my time on the planet was limited, and I wanted to avoid regrets and turn my many, many failures into victories.

But the truth is that it didn't work out that way.

Looking back on things, I can map out my thought process to tidy-up the complex and chaotic jumble of feelings and emotions, but, at the time, I was a confused, scared mess. I was out of my comfort zone and out of my depth.

Did I use this life-changing failure to take that giant leap into my conquer zone? Did I bollocks.

You might have found yourself in a similar situation – maybe not being kicked in the willy by your employers, like I was – but finding yourself at something of a career crossroads, unable to decide which route to take.

Do you take the road of safe, boring comfort, with its pension schemes, coffee meetings, SMART objectives (that's specific, measurable, achievable, realistic and time-bound) and five-year plans? Or do you take the path of discomfort, with all the fear, excitement and butterflies-in-the-tummy nervousness that could ultimately lead you to conquer everything standing before you?

Maybe you genuinely don't know which path to take because you don't know where you want to go. I know there is nothing more frustrating than sitting on the toilet, watching a motivational YouTube marathon, seeing all the gurus telling you to follow your passions and do what you love. That's all very well if you happen to have a deep love for running a coffee shop, artisan baking, drawing or music, but if you have a hidden talent for eating pizza and masturbation, then it's not the most helpful advice.

This was me. No, not the pizza and masturbation (not something to be combined in any way, shape or form). I'm talking about not knowing where to turn.

As my old management-consultancy career lay around me in ruins, I wasn't sure what to do next. I liked sport, but I also liked Heineken and Marlboros, so my Olympic chances were slim. I couldn't draw, bake, play, think, talk, jump or, come to think of it, do any verb well enough to make a career out of it. If I had known what I wanted to do, I would have strapped on a pair of balls, and gone and done it (at least this is what I told myself). But the truth was that I didn't have a clue. Or so I thought.

"What do you love to do?" a wise and very un-fucked-up friend asked me one day.

I pretended to give it some thought for a few minutes, but I had known the answer immediately. The rest of that time, I spent silently asking my comfort zone to shut up because it was telling me that this idea was stupid and open for ridicule. I plucked up the courage eventually, opened my mouth to speak and winced in anticipation of the volley of laugher to be launched at me. "Well… this might sound silly… in fact, it's pretty idiotic. It's just this stupid thing that I've always loved doing, and would love to do more of…"

I stared at the floor as I continued. It was too late to put the genie back in the bottle now. "I kind of love going on adventures… and pushing myself to my mental and physical limits. I believe anyone can do this. I want to face my fears and step out of my comfort zone… and I want to help other people do the same. I want to help people do the things they thought they couldn't do."

As soon as I said these words, I smiled. It was like a colossal weight had been lifted from my shoulders. I lifted my gaze back to my friend, only to see her scrolling through her Instagram feed.

"Jolly good; go and do that then," she said absently. "I'm off to yoga."

Middle-class pep-talk delivered.

In a flurry of excitement, I knew this could be the calling I'd been waiting for. My life finally had purpose. I had goals to deliver, ambitions to realise and dreams to fulfil! I spent the whole day, night and the following day scribbling plans, defining targets and drafting mission statements. I was so motivated and so fired-up that it was impossible to sleep, eat or do anything apart from scheme and plan and strategise. I'd never known an energy and passion like it, and this feeling told me I was on the right path. The scary path, the path of the unknown, and the path on which few dare to tread.

The path to my conquer zone!

Until, that was, my comfort zone had the final word. Like a villain in a James Bond movie who you think is dead but then rises again and tries to extinguish 007 one final time, my badly – but not mortally – wounded comfort zone staggered forward. The same old fears, doubts, *what-ifs* and *yes-buts* started to creep back into my thoughts.

Then, before I knew it, the dream was on hold, and I was collecting my impressively shiny ID badge on the first day of my new role as…

A management consultant, for fuck's sake.

I'd allowed my comfort zone to tell me a bucketful of lies, and I'd stepped away from my passions and my conquer zone once again. But, hey, it wasn't all bad. The pension was decent, and I didn't even have to sell the Porsche.

This pattern continued for almost another three years. In that time, I had three jobs with three different companies, becoming more and more disillusioned each time. I became *certain* that this was not who I was any more. I was convinced that life had something more in store for me. But try as I might, I couldn't escape my comfort zone to discover what it was.

By then, it was January 2019. When I was sitting in a five-hour workshop, staring at a table like a zombie, while an excited discussion buzzed around me regarding how many waste-management employees could be fired from a particular department, I knew I'd had enough.

I slammed my hand down on the table and pressed the fuck-it button.

The fuck-it button is kryptonite to our comfort zones. Although we're not able to see it, we all know that glowing, red button is there, and sometimes the despair, the noise and the shit reverberating around our ears gets so much that we just don't care any more. We reach that tipping point, and we no longer care about comfort. We hit the event-horizon of *enough*. Screw the pension plans, the career ladder and the safety of that twice-yearly weekend in the Cotswolds with those people we hate. This is the moment where we want something even more than comfort. This is the moment we want the real versions of ourselves back. We are ready to lead the lives we were meant to lead.

When I reached this moment and hit the button, I was hit by a strange sense of calm. There was none of the gripping, strangling terror from when I had failed in my job three years earlier. I was almost like a sociopath, feeling no emotion: no elation, fear, nervousness nor terror. I just knew this was the way life had to be. I simply had to escape my comfort zone. There was no other option open to me now.

It was either enter my conquer zone, or live a life of unfulfilled potential and total regret.

*

And this, my friends, is where we say goodbye.

Not a proper goodbye, obviously. Most of you will have noticed that this is not yet the end of the book. Or if it is, it means someone has beaten you to it and ripped out the best pages.

But this is a goodbye to your comfort zone. So far, we have discussed everything you need to be aware of – and take command of – to break free temporarily from those familiar, comforting bonds that keep you from the life and experiences of which you dream.

We have examined our supposed enemy (the comfort zone), why it exists and why it has become such a central part of our modern lives. We have even broken away from tradition and realised that, sometimes, our comfort zones come in handy, and we should actually enjoy some time in them once in a while.

We have realised that living the life we dream of isn't actually about doing certain things, having things, or taking photos of them and putting them on Instagram; it's about *time*. And leaving our comfort zone is essential if we are to, quite simply, have the time of our lives.

What's more, we have ignored the experts, the YouTube motivators and the keyboard warriors who never set foot outside their bedrooms but believe they are qualified to tell you how to leave your comfort zone for good. Then we have looked at the essential elements required to move from being someone who *talks* about making their wildest dreams happen to a person who actually *takes* the leap of faith to make them happen.

We have learned that we need to decide (and then JFDI), recognise we are all mortals who are just renting this time on earth, and make the most of that time, avoiding regret and embracing failure.

By understanding and embracing these elements, you are ready to leave your comfort zone behind. And this is where the tale ends.

For most people.

You see, when people talk about leaving their comfort zone, it is a story of escape. Like *Escape from Alcatraz, The Great Escape* or *Papillion*. Or even *Toy Story*. There is often little focus on *how* to leave our comfort zones (we are told to just accept that comfort zones are bad and don't ask any questions), *where* we are going (success, success everywhere – just pay the guru and think about success), or *what* we are going to do when we get there (pay for the guru's new Ferrari).

We've been told for so long we need to escape our comfort zones that we don't even know *why* we're supposed to do it. But I've just given you the tools you need to understand why a comfort-zone holiday might be good for your mind, body and soul. However, that's only half the story.

We don't get anywhere in life by simply focusing on what we are *leaving* and not giving any thought to where we are *going*. It's like getting out of a warm bed or leaving a steaming-hot shower: you've spent so long building up the courage and telling yourself a story in order to take the difficult and uncomfortable first step, but once you've left that zone, you know it would be *so* easy just to hop backwards, and get right back to where you feel safe and warm.

This is why so many people get the advice about leaving their comfort zones, but then don't know what to do next, so they step right back to where they came from. But not us. Not today.

The second half of this book is going to teach you about how to enter your *conquer zone*, and not only enter it but survive, thrive and do the things you never thought possible. This isn't about taking a tentative step off the high board into the deep, dark and scary lagoon below; this is about taking a running leap, bombing into the water and then splashing around on your back, looking up at the sky, and smiling while blowing water from your mouth and bubbles from your arse.

This is what your conquer zone is all about, and I know this because I went there and I saw what was possible. I didn't go there as an athlete, professionally trained adventurer or special forces solider. I went into my conquer zone as a fucked-up, depressed, heavy-drinking, big-on-dreams-but-short-on-action, ordinary guy.

Now, once more, I'm going back there, and I'm taking you with me.

EIGHT

WELCOME TO THE CONQUER ZONE

The tornado hit with the force of a detonating bomb. Sand, rocks and bits of equipment exploded through the exposed tent like shrapnel. The dust, noise and furious rumbling spread through the earth like an approaching freight train, waking me from my slumber just in time to see one of my companions knocked almost unconscious by the twisted tree trunk that had served as a flimsy tent pole. Seconds later, the whole structure collapsed around us.

In the cold and arid desert night, I desperately screwed my eyes shut against the whirling cyclone of sand. As my ears were filled with confused shouts, panicked screams, and garbled instructions that were shouted in English, French and Arabic, I spat out a mouthful of grit and allowed myself a confused grin.

A few months ago, Thursday mornings would have been spent in the same dull, repetitive, comfortable way. This Thursday, however, I was very much in my conquer zone. At least, I told myself I was.

But at that particular moment, in the middle of the Sahara Desert at 3am, hundreds of miles away from the faintest hint of civilisation, when I was cold, dirty, hungry, exhausted and now finding myself in the unfortunate position of being in the direct path of a tornado, I was beginning to have second thoughts.

A life of normal comfort didn't seem so bad right now.

Yet here I was. In my conquer zone. The place I'd always wanted to be, but was too scared to visit. I'd managed to step away from my comfort zone of being a slightly depressed, unfit, heavy-drinking corporate worker, mainly thanks to using the methods and approaches explained in the first half of this book.

Armed with all this new, fragile confidence – this unfamiliar boldness – I had wanted to do something unique. I'd made the decision to change, I'd accepted that time was limited, and I knew I didn't want a life of regret. Hell, I'd even accepted that I might fail at a few things along the way, and that was OK.

I didn't want to dip my toe into my conquer zone, I needed to jump right in. Should I book a holiday to an exotic destination, take up a new hobby, sign up for a physical challenge or learn a new skill?

All these would have been sensible options, so they were ignored. I chose something altogether different.

The toughest footrace on the planet: a multi-day, self-sufficient ultramarathon through the burning heat of the Sahara Desert.

It's called stepping into the conquer zone for a reason.

The Marathon des Sables is commonly regarded as one of the toughest feats of human endurance. The 200-mile race was devised by a French concert promoter named Patrick Bauer, who decided to venture into a very sandy conquer zone and crossed the Sahara Desert alone in 1984. The first official race took place in 1986, and the race has now evolved to become a six-day ultramarathon where competitors tend to run a marathon every day except for the dreaded 'long day', which consists of a double marathon. Just for the fun of it.

Every year, athletes would be guaranteed to face 1000-metre-high sand dunes; miles of scorching salt plains and beds of razor-sharp rocks; freak tornados; blinding sandstorms; deadly snakes, spiders and scorpions; and temperatures reaching 55 degrees Celsius in the day and plummeting to below freezing at night. No wonder the waiver forms stated that competitors would need insurance to cover the costs of repatriating their bodies in the event of death.

If the race conditions were not hard enough, entrants had to carry all their own food, equipment and clothing on their back; and sleep in makeshift shelters consisting of a ragged blanket propped up by a pointy bit of tree. This was no *Lawrence of Arabia* tour where everyone has a stroll, gets a nice tan and then goes back to the air-conditioned hotel for a gin and tonic by the pool.

Oh, and one more thing: water was rationed. Just for a laugh.

Over the years, this all-consuming race has attracted the world's finest endurance athletes, Olympians and legendary explorers, such as Sir Ranulph Fiennes. In 1994, Italian competitor Mauro Prosperi wandered lost in the desert for 10 days following a sandstorm. Disorientated and alone, he survived only by drinking his own urine, and killing snakes and lizards before eating them raw. When rescue failed to materialise and his outlook appeared hopeless, he gave up on life. After writing a short farewell note to his wife upon a rock with a piece of charcoal, he slit his wrists and waited to die. The only reason he awoke a few hours later was because severe dehydration has caused his blood to thicken and clot in his veins.

Unfortunately, other competitors over the years had not been so lucky and never returned from the desert alive.

This challenge was to be the first step into my conquer zone. It was me – the non-athlete, non-ultrarunner, unfit, non-focused, non-ready office worker – who would be trying to complete this race. From the beginning, I knew the odds were against me. No one believed I could conquer this challenge. But I knew that, if I was going to be successful – if I was going to step into my conquer zone and not just survive but thrive – I would have to do something different.

I knew I would need to think, behave and believe in a different way. I would have to control my thoughts and develop a strategy that would allow me to achieve anything I could imagine. I knew I must develop an unstoppable mindset that would keep me in my conquer zone no matter what the world threw at me, and that would give me the confidence to believe I could make my dreams happen.

Furthermore, I knew if I could develop this roadmap to not only enter my conquer zone but *stay* there, then anyone else could do the same.

THE BURNING DESIRE

I'd never known heat like it. The oppressive temperatures assaulted me from all angles like a surprise ambush. The searing rays of the sun burned relentlessly down upon my head, while fire seemed to rise up from the depths of the earth and radiate through the sand beneath my feet, making me dance a slow, never-ending jig. I was trying to adapt and learn rapidly so I could perform in an environment that was designed to kill me.

Standing on the starting line of the 33rd Marathon des Sables, I reflected on my decision to run this race, and remembered how it could have been so different.

*

"You're going to kill yourself you stupid fucking dickhead." My wife wouldn't win any awards for her motivational speaking, but I couldn't fault her logic.

I had chosen a nondescript night in February to share my news. Sitting in comfort on our sofa, with discarded pizza boxes and crisp wrappers around our feet, and some mindless TV show failing to distract us from our phones, I had decided to toss in a grenade.

"So… I was thinking, I'd like to enter the world's toughest race," I ventured.

"That thing in the Sahara Desert?" She laughed. "Great idea; I assume you've got a death wish?"

"Well… it's not that I'd *like* to enter the race," I continued timidly. "I've actually applied, and it seems that I've been accepted."

WELCOME TO THE CONQUER ZONE

"You're bloody stupid," she repeated. As her laugher transformed into a look of serious concern, I started to get the message. "That is a *proper* race. For *proper* athletes. You did a marathon when you were five years younger, and it almost bloody killed you! Why on earth do you want to try this now?"

"Because I believe I can do it," I replied quietly.

Entering this race hasn't exactly been on a whim. I'd had my eye on it for a while; for years, in fact. I'd been one of those people who would read all the articles, watch the videos, follow the social media accounts, and bore anyone who would listen about the race stats, facts and figures. In fact, I'd do absolutely anything regarding this race...

Except actually enter it.

But then, one day, I knew enough was enough. I decided to do it. I realised *time* was short, and I no longer wanted to live a life of *regret*. Even though I was terrified of *failure*, I knew I could no longer let it stop me from realising my dreams. So, I knew I had to hit the *fuck-it button*.

That's why, on that normal lunchtime during a standard working day in a beige office building on a grey February day, I took out my credit card and signed up for the race. My comfort zone had been well and truly left behind, and a surge of adrenaline and pride flowed through my veins.

Followed by panic, terror and an urge to vomit.

As my wife confirmed helpfully that evening, I knew I wasn't fit enough, strong enough, fast enough or prepared enough. But despite all the odds being stacked against me, and every logical argument telling me to pick up the phone, claim that a criminal endurance athlete had stolen my credit card and gone on the world's healthiest crime spree, and ask for a refund, I knew I had one thing in my favour: a burning desire to succeed.

If you don't start with a burning desire, then don't start. So much time, money, energy, stress and brainpower has been wasted by people who have started something but didn't have that burning desire to see it through. People leave their comfort zones and start things, which is great, but they often start for the wrong reasons.

People will watch the YouTube videos about breaking free from their comfort zones, and they manage to do this, but then they go to the wrong place. They go to a place they *think* is cool, will make them money, will impress someone, or will earn them love, attention, respect or power. This does not take them to their conquer zones.

The conquer zone can only be reached when we have a burning desire to get there. If we don't have this, then we won't be willing to make the personal, physical and mental sacrifices. I'm not talking about leaving comfort behind forever and proving to the world how you don't need sleep, food, your family or love in order to pursue your goals relentlessly. That would be unrealistic and bloody stupid. But in order to get the things you've never *had* before, you're going to need to do the do the things you've never *done* before. And this is going to be uncomfortable and difficult and a bit scary at times. In order to tolerate this, you're going to need a burning desire to push past the discomfort in order to get to your conquer zone.

And I had a burning desire to run the world's toughest race.

It was this burning desire that got me out of bed on the Saturday morning after I'd booked my place in the Marathon des Sables, and hauled my sweating, wheezing, nauseated arse round my first parkrun in 31 minutes. It was also the burning desire that made me think twice about sparking up a cigarette and going to the pub immediately afterwards.

It was the burning desire that got me running five miles a week, then 10, then 20, then 40, until, miraculously, it seemed normal to run 10 miles on a Monday, 10 more on the Wednesday, the same again on the Friday, and then a cheeky marathon on the Sunday. And, believe me, no one was more surprised by this transformation than I was. Before this metamorphosis, there would be a greater chance of me running for Miss World than running over 50 miles a week on a regular basis. But I was only able to keep going, and to continue pushing myself forwards through pulled muscles, knee strains, back spasms, swollen ankles and a scratched eyeball (running like a pro – headlong into a low-hanging tree branch at night), because I had the burning desire. That burning desire got me out of the house in darkness, snow, stinging hail and driving rain. It got me out of the door, day after day, when all I wanted to do was put my feet up and stay inside in comfort.

The burning desire made me smile quietly when people laughed at my decision to run this race. For someone who had lived so much of his life based on what would make others happy, and through a fear of being different, laughed at or judged, it gave me confidence and courage where before there had been none. The burning desire gave me inner strength when people mocked me and told me there was no hope in hell of me completing the challenge. The burning desire kept me calm when my friends became angry and verbally abusive, telling me I was stupid and was going to come back in a body bag. The burning desire helped me keep a straight face when my *MABQ* colleague actually went to the trouble of preparing a PowerPoint presentation to highlight all the reasons why my attempt was doomed to failure.

It was the burning desire that had led me to actually *do* the thing I'd always wanted to do in order to get into my conquer zone. It also gave me the clarity to realise that we so often kid ourselves and try to do the opposite.

My friendly co-worker *MABQ* has been a prime example of this. With his sweat patches, tight trousers and fondness for telling me why I would fail, he had developed a habit of doing obstacle-course races (or OCRs, as he insisted on calling them). These OCRs became the topic of every conversation. It didn't matter whether people in the office were discussing the weather, Brexit, climate change or even – as a last resort – *work*, somehow, *MABQ* would always manage to turn the conversation towards Spartans, nuclear races, rope climbs, Z-walls, Hercules hoists and spear throws. *MABQ* would always boast proudly about how he was 'smashing out of his comfort zone'.

Except, he wasn't.

By deciding to do nothing except get muddy and be a bit of a dick to everyone, *MABQ* was actually making himself more and more *comfortable*. In fact, his comfort zone had managed to construct a story whereby he *believed* he was challenging himself, but, actually, he was getting more and more settled.

We've already seen how our brains are amazing at adaptation. The upside of this is that we can slowly mould and shape ourselves to fit our circumstances and gradually transform something uncomfortable into something altogether more pleasant. The downside is that – without a burning desire to keep changing, improving and challenging ourselves – we will *always* shift back into our comfort zones, whether we like it or not.

No matter what society defines as 'stepping out of your comfort zone' – public speaking, climbing a mountain, flying a space shuttle, asking someone on a date, abseiling into an active volcano or going to the supermarket while wearing a facemask – if you do it every day, it will become normal. This is why we all freak out when we think about open heart surgery, but a surgeon with 40 years' experience can yawn and moan about the price of flights to the Seychelles this winter while he slices your chest, cracks open your ribcage, and clears a lifetime of bacon and Big Macs from the arteries of your heart. What's uncomfortable to one person is someone else's bread and butter.

This is why we need to have the burning desire to change our lives. We need that push to keep moving forwards, because if we stand still, then our world stops moving, and we stop growing. So many gurus make the mistake of talking about 'breaking out of your comfort zone' as being a one-time thing, like escaping from prison. It isn't. If you leave your comfort zone, and just go and sit somewhere else, then, before you know it, you've just constructed a brand new comfort zone there. But to enter your conquer zone, you need a burning desire to take a leap of faith and face the unknown.

*

Standing on that start line, however, with helicopters buzzing only metres above my head, throwing a burning salvo of sand and dust into my eyes and mouth, I had a different kind of burning desire. I wanted to cry, and I wanted to be anywhere else in the world right then. Preferably, somewhere where the early morning temperature was lower than 39 degrees Celsius.

The race organiser, Patrick Bauer, climbed unsteadily atop the roof of a 4x4 truck to address the athletes. And me. As he hailed the competitors excitedly in French, a translator (looking equally French in a pair of pink jeans and a black turtleneck sweater – in the middle of the desert) struggled to keep up with the multiple occurrences of '*allez*' and 'supercool' being thrown around with abandon. He need not have bothered: the helicopters circling overhead, like a scene from Operation Desert Storm, made it impossible to understand what was being said in either language.

In that calm before the storm, I took the opportunity to glance around at my fellow racers. I spotted the North Africans, with their chiselled faces and wiry muscles not carrying an extra ounce of fat. Born and raised in this harsh, unforgiving landscape, their bodies had been moulded and honed into pure instruments of desert endurance racing. They stood calmly, with broad smiles plastered across their faces, totally at home and at peace with what the next six days would bring. Even though this was a familiar environment to them, I pondered that these individuals were still looking for new ways to enter their conquer zones. Many of these Moroccans, Algerians and Egyptians had run this race before – some had even won it – yet they still possessed a burning desire to push their limits and step out of their comfort zones once more.

Standing alongside these lithe and spirited desert ultrarunners was an altogether different creature: Marcus, the fund manager from Surrey. His £130 Lycra compression t-shirt struggled to contain the bulge of his stomach as it poured over the waistband of his equally tight running shorts. He puffed out his cheeks and wiped the back of one hand across a pale and slick forehead, with the grease from his St Tropez sunscreen already merging into the rivers of sweat cascading down his face in the dawn heat. With his other hand, he simultaneously fiddled with his Global Positioning System (GPS) watch, GoPro camera, heart-rate-monitor strap and smart phone.

On the surface, all the competitors had nothing in common. They had different lives, upbringings, careers, religious beliefs and bank balances. They almost certainly had different futures ahead of them. But, at that moment, they shared a common desire and a united goal: they wanted to enter their conquer zones and push themselves to their limits. They wanted to see what they were really capable of, and recognised that this moment would be imprinted on their minds until their dying day.

Every single one of the competitors who surrounded me brought their own backstory, circumstances and reason for being present on that lonely, desolate patch of sand. There was the woman who had quit her safe corporate career and opted for a life no longer driven by financial gain, so as to inspire her daughters and other young girls to dream big and pursue their goals relentlessly; the middle-aged housewife who had escaped an abusive relationship and wanted to embark upon this challenge as a reason to get fit and show her body-shaming ex-partner that she was more powerful than he could ever have imagined; the man who had been diagnosed with stage-four terminal cancer, but who had chosen to spend a few of his precious last days away from his loved ones and with a bunch of strangers in the desert to raise money for a prostate cancer charity; and the amputee and the blind runner who were in the desert to show they were empowered and not limited by their physical attributes.

Plus there were runners from Tokyo who were embarking on the race dressed as emojis and wearing traditional Japanese *geta* sandals, consisting of blocks of wood. There's stepping into your conquer zone, and then there's being fucking crazy.

What united each of us, however, had been the burning desire to step away from comfort and into our conquer zones. We all had our different reasons for being at the start line, and we had all experienced a different journey to lead us to that moment. But here we were, all united in our belief that, by pushing our bodies and minds to the limits, we could enter our conquer zones and change our lives forever.

I considered how my life could have been so different and how I could have made so many other micro-decisions that might have led me on a different path. Would I be here on the start line if my dad hadn't died? If I hadn't failed in my corporate job? If I hadn't decided to change my life? If I'd decided to stay in a warm, comfy bed on that very first day of training instead of embarking on a parkrun?

The questions and *what-ifs* were blown away by the first chords of AC/DC's 'Highway to Hell' being blasted over an assembly of loudspeakers. The race started, and my own highway to hell had just begun.

NINE

BACK TO SCHOOL

Why couldn't she just close the bloody window?

I buried my head deeper under the duvet in the vain hope of hiding from the outside world forever. I had no idea what time it was; the only thing I could wrap my foggy and befuddled head around was the memory of a fitful and broken sleep. And, thanks to my wife leaving the bedroom window open, an icy wind was somehow stealing into the warm confines of my bedding like a silent ninja.

Sighing as the realisation dawned that sleep was abandoning me, and the big, bad, fully conscious world would soon be here, I wiggled and wrapped one arm around my surprisingly thin pillow as if it were the shoulders of a long-lost friend after a night on the ale. My other hand reached out lazily and caressed the cold and gritty shoulders of my wife.

One eye opened.

My wife's skin was usually impeccably silky smooth and moisturised, not coarse, loose and grainy. Come to think of it, my pillow was normally deep, enveloping and comforting, not rough, hard and wafer-thin, like a piece of cardboard that had been folded in on itself numerous times.

Something was wrong.

I prised open my second eye, and was greeted by a new dawn in a devilishly inhospitable landscape.

As I unfurled my numb and stiff body into something resembling a seated position, I rubbed my hands over my face and gazed at my reality. Rather than my comforting dream of being enveloped in a cosy bed with my wife, with the cold breeze rushing through the window, I was now awake and faced with an entirely different prospect.

I was surrounded by sand, grit and gravel, a handful of which I'd scooped up when reaching out for my imaginary spouse. And, similar to an ill-advised encounter with an off-duty air-hostess in Ibiza back in 1999, I'd discovered that sand really did get *everywhere*. The luxuriously soft and enveloping duvet and pillow I'd been dreaming of turned out to be a thin sleeping bag and an inflatable pillow no bigger than a saucer. The breeze waking me was not from an open window but was the cold desert wind cutting through the open sides of our tent. Although calling it a 'tent' was overly generous; it was more of a moth-eaten blanket, ragged and tattered from decades of being hauled around the desert, and suspended five feet from the stony ground by a gnarled tree branch.

Surrounding me like six giant slugs were the bodies of my tent mates, who were wrapped in their sleeping bags and huddled together for warmth against the bitter desert night. As they stirred, a dawn chorus of farts, moans, groans and belches greeted my ears. To escape the smell of bodies that had last been washed three days ago in the UK, I poked my head out of the open side of the tent, and my mouth dropped open in wonder at the world around me.

The camp was sitting in the middle of a large dust bowl stretching five miles in every direction. Around 100 identical black tents – each fashioned from a similar ragged blanket supported by a single stick – had been erected in a formation of three circles. In the very centre of the camp, the ashes from the previous night's fire were still smouldering, like the smudge of a nucleus inside an atom of sand. The inner circle housed the elite athletes: the world's finest ultrarunners, who had proudly pinned their national flags and the emblems of their corporate sponsors to the outsides of their tents. The middle circle of tents housed a collection of nationalities from all corners of the globe. I was intrigued by the small cultural quirks and idiosyncrasies each country portrayed: the Spanish athletes would collect small sticks and twigs diligently to create a communal fire for cooking; the Italians put such emphasis on food that each runner carried a different ingredient in their backpack in order to combine them together and create a delicious dish every evening; the Japanese cleared every stray stone, twig and ball of desert-critter shit meticulously away from their tents, and smoothed the sand with their hands until it was as immaculate as a freshly vacuumed carpet; and the French, on the other hand, thought nothing of strolling around the camp naked, which I discovered when I was treated to the view of a full-on Gallic morning glory.

Finally, the outer ring of the camp housed the Brits. Segregated into our own little colonial corner of the desert, the representatives of the UK were kept safely away from the rest of the world. It was perhaps not the greatest ever coincidence that the toilets were also situated directly next to the British tents and furthest away from the heart of the camp.

'Toilet' was perhaps too grand a word. If you wanted to picture the exact *opposite* of a comfort zone, this would be it. In reality, the 'toilet' was actually a plastic toilet seat attached to a wobbly wooden stool. At the start of the race, I had been handed a small handful of brown bags by a grinning race marshal.

"Poo bags!" he said, a little too excitedly. Perhaps he was thinking about the proper toilets, electricity, running water, bar, Wi-Fi and air conditioning on offer in the 'race marshal and media' camp that sat half a mile away.

As I stowed my poo bags safely in a corner of my backpack, I realised that I wouldn't exactly be needing an instruction manual. When the call of nature arose, all we had to do was step out of our tents, enter the 'toilet', stretch the open bag around the toilet seat, perch on the stool and look up at the deep-marine-blue sky.

This was fine until the bag fell off the seat and the freshly deposited contents fell onto your shorts and socks. Or until the desert wind whipped up the flimsy plastic sheeting surrounding the toilet, treating the whole camp to a pasty, white, full-moon arse display. Or if, despite your best efforts, while trying to perch delicately on the seat, you toppled off the thing altogether, grabbing at and pulling down the plastic walls of the cubicle, leaving you exposed and stranded on your back in the sand with your legs waving in the air, like an overturned, shitty-arsed beetle.

Indeed, there was nothing like being close to the toilets that made us question the UK's current reputation in the world.

But the chaos and disgustingness of the toilets would always be forgotten in an instant when I looked around in awe at the beauty of my environment. Sand dunes embraced and wrapped around each other in a cocktail of yellows, oranges, browns and greys. Deep cracks criss-crossed parched riverbeds, and, in the distance, proud, black monolithic mountains protruded from the desert floor like a fortress blocking our path. It felt as if we had awoken on a distant, desert planet, which was unforgiving and hostile, as if the entire landscape regarded us as alien intruders and was desperate to rid us from its surface. It was intimidating, brutal and utterly majestic.

My wondrous gaze was broken by the kerfuffle of the tent being dismantled around me. The local Bedouin tribespeople had no time to stop for the niceties of, "Would you mind awfully if we took the tent down now?" or "Would you prefer us to come back after you've got dressed?" They had a job to do, and all they cared about was getting it done.

Steve, the helpful British race organiser called by to check we were OK. "All right, guys, are you ready for today?" he asked.

"Not really," I replied, trying to sound more confident than I felt.

"Ah, you'll be fine," he said with a smile. "But you *do* know how to deal with the harsh conditions today, don't you?"

"Er... no," I responded, a little more cautiously.

"Handling difficult terrain?"

"Nope."

"Water management? Technical climbs? Using your distress flare? Manipulating your venom pump? Compass skills? Basic signals? Emergency comms? Sandstorm procedures?"

"I think I might have missed some of that," I croaked in barely a whisper.

Steve threw back his head and laughed. "*I hope you're not scared of needles then!*" he shouted to make himself heard above the growing roar of rotor blades as the helicopters took to the sky. "Everyone is allowed one rehydration IV [intravenous] drip; if you need a second, you'll be out of the race. Not that you'll care by that stage… because you'll be fucked!"

I rushed to put on my dusty and sweat-stained clothes, and stuff my few possessions into my backpack before they were blown away by the downdraft and following sandblast.

Welcome to race-day two.

IT'S NOT WHAT YOU KNOW

Stepping into our conquer zones is stepping into the unknown. It means making a conscious decision to go somewhere where we *know* we don't currently have the skills or abilities to make life easy for ourselves.

Anyone considering leaving their comfort zone to try a new challenge should be applauded. However, when confronted with the difficulties of the new task, they tend to fall into two camps:

1. **Intimidated and overwhelmed.** These are the brave souls who were inspired to step out of their comfort zones, and they went and bloody did it. They got the inspiration, made the decision, closed their eyes and stepped forwards into the unknown…

    And then realised they lacked the skills to complete their challenge and told themselves it was impossible while hopping back into their comfort zone, like a holiday bather who dips a toe into the freezing-cold swimming pool before deciding quickly that life on the sun lounger, sipping a Sex on the Beach while fantasising about the lifeguard is much more preferable.

This is the person who always kind of thought a new challenge would be tricky, but didn't take the time to research or understand what it would actually entail. When the brutal reality smacks them in the face, they start to realise that they don't like this new feeling of the unknown. This tiny, little opening in their consciousness is all the comfort zone needs to shove its foot in the door and start the campaign to entice that individual back into the safety of what they've always known.

Not everyone is intimidated by a new challenge. Some people, to coin a phrase, *feel the fear and do it anyway*. But, sometimes, doing it anyway is the worst idea in the world. These people are suffering from…

2. **Blind bravery.** That's a nice way of saying *blind stupidity*. These fine characters are at the polar opposite end of the scale to the *intimidated and overwhelmed,* and are much more dangerous. Anyone who has been cornered at a party by the self-crowned king (because they are usually male) of skiing/golf/hiking/triathlon/ scuba diving/CrossFit knows that pride often comes before a painful fall.

   The sufferer of blind bravery has no problem taking a running leap from their comfort zone, and they'll make sure everyone knows about it. The only problem is that they'll land nowhere near their conquer zone. They pay no heed to what skills they need, the advice to ask for or the guidance they should seek. The only thing that appeals is diving in without a second thought, and to hell with the consequences.

   There is only one thing more perilous to one's dream than not having the courage to try, and that is when too much courage turns into stupidity. Consider the following statements:

Person A: "I'd really love to do that, but I don't think I can. I just wouldn't have a clue what to do."
Person B: "I have no fucking idea, but everyone else makes it look easy. Just fake it till you make it, right? *YOLO!*"

How many times do you think a Person A has been seriously injured or killed by the challenge they were contemplating? Not many. And how many Person Bs would you find the local morgue? Very many.

And this is why the conundrum of escaping our comfort zones is not a hokey-cokey issue. It's not about being totally *in* or *out* of your comfort zone. It's about making the right choices, minimising the risks you face, and backing yourself to overcome the challenges you wish to tackle.

In the build-up to the Marathon des Sables, I met both types of people. I came across the uncommitted and doubtful naysayers who admitted they would love to complete the challenge – except for the fact they couldn't run, hated the heat, couldn't pack a backpack and had no idea how to plan their nutrition. I also met the individuals who scoffed at my challenge and thought it was a 'walking holiday', a 'con for middle-class people' and also a 'massive gay waste of time'. Nope, I don't know why the homophobic insult crept in there either. I guess some people *really* don't like it when you cause them to start questioning their own comfort zones.

For those first few months after booking my place in the race, I became the epitome of what I have now christened the 'comfort-cokey'. Some days I was *in,* almost paralysed by self-doubt, and overwhelmed by my lack of fitness, experience and knowledge. Other days I was *out,* propping up the bar, beer in hand, arrogantly telling anyone who would listen it was, "just a little jog in the desert".

What I was afraid to admit – at times, even to myself – was that I was scared. I didn't know what I didn't know, and when I did discover I didn't know something, I didn't know how to know about it.

Brain scrambled? Yep, that's how I felt as I lay in bed staring at the ceiling every single night, feeling a rope of panic wrapping tighter and tighter around my chest.

But then I discovered there was a way through the comfortable, confusing mists of the journey towards my conquer zone. There were no shortcuts, no bypasses. There was only one way, and it was the long way.

BACKING YOURSELF

Race-day minus nine months.

Anyone who has been involved with planning a wedding knows the feeling. It's the tipping point. It's the moment when stress outweighs excitement. It's the very second your mindset shifts from, "This is going to be the best day of our lives" to "Fuuuck, *nothing* will be done in time! *Why did we ever say yes to this stupid thing in the first place?*"

This was the feeling that was crushing me as I sat on my bedroom floor, with discarded running shoes, energy bars, dehydrated food, water bottles and five different types of sunscreen strewn around me, like collateral damage from a detonated ultramarathon grenade.

It's fair to say I was panicking, but then I did something different. Despite the loud protests from my comfort zone – telling me I was boring, worrying about nothing or overthinking things – I got a pen and a piece of paper, and started on a different path. And this, dear reader, is how you too can shift from panic disguised as comfort to actually embarking on the challenge you desire.

1. KNOW WHAT YOU DON'T KNOW

It sounds simple, but, so often, we don't know what we don't know. Now, this carries both advantages and disadvantages. On the bright side, when stepping out of our comfort zones, we can be in blissful ignorance, and fully unaware of our gross lack of skills and capabilities, a bit like the time I was snorkelling merrily on the Great Barrier Reef, unaware a three-metre bull shark was circling slowly and eyeing me up as it decided whether to have my feet as an appetiser, or just paddle in and gobble me up head first. I, on the other hand, was none the wiser because I was not aware of the full situation, just my sheltered, goggled view of what was directly in front of me.

On the downside, however, being unaware of the skills and capabilities we require can be paralyzingly daunting. Taking the snorkelling incident again, if I had decided to not go into the water because I wasn't an expert in the topographical features of the nearby reef, ocean currents, free-diving techniques and local marine life, not to mention how to fight a hungry shark, I would never have taken the plunge. I would have forever stayed in my comfort zone on the boat, making excuses about not being quite ready or the conditions not being quite right.

I found the most effective way to understand the skills required to step into my conquer zone for any particular challenge was to try to learn from the experts. Sometimes, this must involve swallowing some pride and accepting that you're not Billy Big-Bollocks, tapping someone on the shoulder, and saying, "I've never done this before, and you appear to be very good at it. Please will you tell me what I need to know and what I need to do."

Nine times out of 10, they will point you in the right direction. And as for the one time out of 10, who wants to take advice from someone who is too busy, arrogant or idle to help?

It's not just about asking one person, it's about doing your wider research. It's not exciting or sexy, but, whatever it is you want to do, you can guarantee at least one person has done something similar and written a blog or a book about it, created an e-course, or is willing to relieve you of your money by some other method in order to tell you all about it. There will be resources out there to help. Just be thankful that you no longer live in in 1985 and have to trudge all the way to the library to borrow a book to read about the subject.

You have no reason to suffer in ignorance. You've done the hard thing by committing to yourself that you will do this challenge, now all you need to do is research the skills you need to complete it. And here's a final tip I've learned from bitter experience: this research should be fun! You should be trying to lap up knowledge like a cat with a saucer of cream. If this all feels a bit like a pain in the arse, may I suggest that you've embarked on a challenge to impress other people, not to step into your conquer zone and fulfil your wildest dreams?

2. EMBRACE IT, STUPID

But, *obviously*, this isn't you. You're undertaking this challenge because you've held a lifelong desire to do it. You've plucked up the courage to start the journey, and now, thanks to your research, you understand your complete lack of skill and stupidity. Congratulations, you've graduated from *no fucking idea how to do it* to *complete fucking lack of ability*.

Progress!

After booking my ticket to the desert, I had felt overwhelmed by the information, resources and self-styled 'experts' who were willing to dish out advice. I'd tried to soak this all up like a sponge, and, before long, I was confident in the knowledge that I had no fucking idea what I was doing. But at least I knew I was starting at zero. I decided to do a stocktake of the skills I needed, and I scored myself against them. It looked a bit like this:

- Running ability: 3/10 (I'd staggered round a marathon… five years ago)
- Desert survival skills: 0/10 (I'd seen a Bear Grylls programme where he squeezed out liquid from camel shit and drank it)
- Heat acclimatisation: 0/10 (North West England was *not* twinned with the north of Western Sahara for a reason)
- Navigation: 3/10 (I'd spent three years at university drinking my way through a geography degree)
- Outdoor skills and camp craft: 0/10 (that was very simple – I fucking hated camping)

On the surface, this was worrying. In fact, under the surface, this was pretty worrying as well. But I also knew I had to start somewhere.

Starting at zero was better than starting from "I have no bloody idea".

In my attempts to learn, research and move my skills from zero to, well, one, I tried to speak to the experts, attend the seminars and bought the tickets for the expos. It's amazing how many people are willing to take your money to tell you things you never knew you needed to know.

I entered a confusing world of ultrarunning, extreme expeditions and endurance sport – and everyone seemed to be a self-styled fountain of knowledge. For a while, I tried the 'fake it till you make it' approach, bluffing my way through discussions and nodding with a mock furrowed brow of empathy while one 'expert' told me of their training schedule of running through the Abu Dhabi desert while wearing a 10kg bulletproof vest.

"Yes, yes," I agreed, and nodded. "That's really similar to my own training plan."

The truth was that I thought it was the most bloody ridiculous thing I'd ever heard. I'd lived in Liverpool for ten years, so I was no stranger to a bulletproof vest or two, but wearing one through the heat of a desert in the Middle East sounded, quite frankly, insane.

I realised my lack of knowledge was starting to get to me. My comfort zone was creeping closer, whispering that my skills gap was too great to bridge. It told me I was just *too* bad at too many things, and I wouldn't be able to fool everyone forever.

So, I stopped trying to fool people.

I embraced my stupidity. I held my hands up and declared I didn't have a fucking clue what I was doing, but I was willing to learn and I was willing to change. I realised that the biggest barrier wasn't actually my lack of knowledge, but it was my fear of looking stupid to people I didn't know who I perceived knew more than me. Once I embraced this and started to speak to fellow competitors openly and honestly, many of them opened up and admitted they didn't really know what they were doing either. And they were pretty scared about it.

So, I found strength in stupidity, and I realised no one really cared how much or how little knowledge I had, as they were too preoccupied with fooling people that they weren't shitting themselves quietly at their own total lack of expertise.

Even though it was the last thing I wanted to do at times, I allowed myself to be honest about my lack of skills. And once I had found that freedom, all I needed was to do something about it.

3. LEARNING YOUR WAY

If you judge a shark on its ability to climb a tree, it will never be successful. If you judge a monkey purely on whether it is the baddest motherfucker in the ocean, it will always be viewed as a failure. We all have different skills, strengths and attributes, so why do we all have to approach a challenge the same way?

Embracing our stupidity and understanding what we need to learn in order to conquer the challenges we face is only half the battle. The real struggle is mastering these new skills to a suitable proficiency in order to get us where we need to be.

When I was trying to wrap my head around all the abilities I would need to gain in order to run 200 miles through the Sahara Desert and survive, I was reminded of Rhodri. Rhodri was a kid in my class when I was 11 years old. Everyone knows a Rhodri.

Rhodri was a learning *machine*. He was an absolute supercomputer. His parents should have christened him 'Hal' or 'T-1000'. He was one of those annoying people who just *got* everything. He didn't need to study for tests, understood every topic of every subject first time, and could hear a piece of music once and then play it on the piano. For him, learning was effortless. He wasn't even arrogant about it; this ability just came as naturally as blinking or sneezing.

At around the same time, I was face down and wailing on my bed, kicking my feet against the mattress and hammering my head against the pillow, as if I were in some kind of deranged ultimate fighting championship (UFC) brawl, all because I couldn't remember the answer to eight times six. This was when I realised that I was not a Rhodri.

While preparing for the Marathon des Sables, I was overcome

by that familiar sense of violent panic. It was the kind of irrational, primitive outburst that comes over us when we are playing a boardgame where we either don't understand the rules or realise we are facing a challenge we can never win. Our comfort zone kicks back against this affront to our pleasant pastime, and we react by swiping the whole game off the table and storming out of the room in tears. Or, as we used to call it in my house: Christmas Day.

I tried everything I could think of to learn the necessary skills in order to undertake my race across the desert. Thankfully, as always, there were plenty of people willing to take my money in order to help me. There were *almost* as many people wanting to share their opinion and tell me how easy they were finding everything as well.

"You need to read this book!" they would say. So I would read it, but not feel any the wiser.

"You need to attend this seminar." So I'd buy a ticket, but everything I heard contradicted what I read in the book.

"You need to get a coaching session from this person." So I'd enquire about coaching, only for the 'coach' to try to sell me his 'training programme', which apparently involved getting drunk in the woods and sharing a small tent together.

The more I tried to learn and the more advice I sought out, the more confused and panicked I got. Then it started to feel like everyone around me was finding it so damn *easy*. It was like I was 11 years old again, sitting in a classroom full of Rhodris, and beating myself up in frustration that I couldn't understand what was wrong with me and why I didn't just *get it*.

Without realising it at the time, I was creating the perfect conditions for my comfort zone to sneak into my life. I'd left the door of my conscience open just wide enough, and now my comfort zone was sneaking in like a thief in the night. It whispered everything I wanted to hear: "You were brave enough to wonder if you *should* do it and stupid enough to think you *could* do it."

The temptation to quit had never been greater. I told myself I could still walk away with my head held high. People would understand.

"It's OK; ultrarunning isn't really your *thing*, anyway," they would say as they handed me a consolatory beer.

Then I thought, *Fuck it. I'm not ready to quit yet.* If I wanted to enter my conquer zone, I'd have to do the tough things, the things I didn't want to do. The hard, boring, frustrating stuff. After all, running through the Sahara Desert wasn't going to be a peaceful stroll, so why did I expect the preparation to be so easy?

We humans learn in different ways. Some of us learn by reading, others by observing and many of us learn by *doing*. To some extent, it doesn't matter which of these methods we use, the important thing is that we do *something*. Don't be the student who can't study before their desk is tidy, the lights aren't too bright, the outside noise is low and the planet Jupiter is in ascendance. Just bloody start. Right now. Training our brains is the same as exercising our bodies: anything is better than nothing.

While you should recognise and understand what works best for you in terms of learning (and to hell with everyone else; if you absorb information best while doing handstands in your underwear, then go do it), nothing beats practice.

If we're not careful, we can use learning as an excuse to step back into our comfort zones because we have the convenient excuse of *not being quite ready*. You will never be 100%, perfectly ready.

I could have read 1,000 books on endurance racing, done a PhD in desert climatology, and watched *Dune* on repeat for a month, and none of these things would have done much to prepare me for a week of running through the searing desert. But these activities would have been straightforward, and they would have given me the *comfort* that I was doing something towards my goal, when – in reality – I was just wasting my time.

Eventually, I chose to do what – if I'm honest with myself – I knew I should have done from the start; I just hadn't wanted to. I spoke to a few experts who had done the race before, thumbed through a couple of books and articles on the Marathon des Sables, and went to bed.

The next day, when the world was still sleeping, and when I would have given a kidney for an extra five minutes of hibernation in my bed, I scraped the ice off my car and drove off into the darkness. Two hours later, the spreading rays from the rising sun illuminated my running shoes as my frozen fingers struggled and fumbled with my laces. I looked out across the deserted, untouched sand and realised I could have been at any time in history in that particular moment. After all, no one in their right mind would seek out a barren beach on the north-west coast of the UK on a frozen February morning.

It was at this point that I realised there is no substitute for learning by *doing*. To commence. To begin. To try. Even though you are painfully aware of your own awkwardness, and almost crippled by your lack of capabilities, the first step of your learning journey is another giant leap towards your conquer zone.

4. AVOIDING PERFECTION

If we successfully complete a task 99 times but then mess it up once, we tend to dwell on the one failure instead of focusing on all the victories we have achieved. When trying to learn something new in order to step into our conquer zone, this feeling is amplified because the learning curve is so much steeper.

To prepare myself for the desert, I thought things would be simple: sure, I'd have to learn a few survival and navigation skills, but I knew I could run, and I was confident I could deal with the heat. Wrong.

I'd identified what I didn't know (everything) and the best way I could learn these skills (ask people to assume I was a three-year-old and explain everything 100 times), and now all I had to do was go and get the knowledge, and I'd be ready to cover the vast, scorching sand as lithely as a desert cobra.

The only problem was that I was shit at everything. Really, really shit.

I had my training plan and I knew what I needed to do; the only issue was that I was terrible at it *all*. I couldn't run while wearing a backpack without my leg muscles screaming out in agony, I would constantly try to navigate with an upside-down map, I'd pass out in saunas (never a wise move in the seedy leisure centres I could afford to frequent), and when I tried to have a poo in a deserted patch of beach, I toppled over and rolled down a sand dune with my pants around my ankles.

I'd huff and puff, and moan and groan, berating myself constantly for my lack of progress, and cursing my luck at being unable to complete what seemed like the simplest task. One night, when I was busy slamming doors in frustration and pondering whether to kick the cat down the stairs, I grumbled to no one in particular, "Why can't anything just go to plan?"

Then I realised there is only one way for life to go to plan, and that's by staying in our comfort zones, which was the very place I was trying to escape.

By moving into my conquer zone, I had to open myself up to failure. I needed to accept that my training wasn't going to go to plan, and my skills would take endless learning and practice just to reach 'not terrible', let alone 'passable'. There was never going to be a perfect time to start learning, there was never a perfect time to take a break, and I would never be perfectly ready for this race. This was never going to change, so I just had to accept it. The only thing I could try to be perfect at was accepting my situation.

Trying to chase perfection, I realised, was wasting time and energy. The only thing it was doing was making me feel shit about myself. And when I felt shit, my comfort zone would come calling, trying to coax me back inside, as if I were a child who had made the mistake of playing outside during a lockdown. Yes, I *know* children don't play outside any more because there are supposedly child molesters hiding on every street corner and it's impossible to get a Wi-Fi signal on their iPads, but it's a quaint way to tell a story.

Anyway, I knew that perfection was pointless. And, in fact, perfection was the *last* thing I wanted. During the race – or whatever challenge you choose to undertake, in fact – things were not going to go perfectly. Things would break, wrong turns would be taken and unexpected stuff would happen – and the best way to prepare mentally for these unforeseen eventualities is to have shit happen in a safe, controlled environment.

If my ankles started to swell after running through 8km of sand, my contact lenses melted to my eyeballs once the temperatures hit 50 degrees Celsius, or I always fell over while having a poo outdoors, it was always better to learn about it *beforehand*. This way, I was able to learn, adapt and create coping strategies. By aiming for practice, not perfection, when stuff went wrong in the middle of the desert, I would be able to react calmly, rather than having a massive meltdown.

So, to step into my conquer zone, I discovered perfection was actually the last thing I needed. I *wanted* shit to go wrong; I wanted to be challenged, overwhelmed and almost broken. Because this is how we learn and grow, and this is how we develop thin layers of confidence. These layers are built up slowly over time until they grow into a suit of armour that will protect us when we embark upon our challenge.

5. RECORDING PROGRESS

Accepting that you're not going to achieve perfection is one thing, but that doesn't stop progress being really bloody *tough* sometimes.

As I tried to train for the ultramarathon that would carry me through the hottest place on earth – by running around my park on a dark and frosty February morning – I couldn't help but stop and ask myself: "What's the bloody point?"

The utterance of these words was all my comfort zone needed to come charging in and fire questions at my conscience like an interrogator from a spy movie.

- Why are you bothering?
- Why aren't you making progress?
- Why are you still so unfit?
- Why isn't it getting any easier?

It would have been so easy to not only listen to these words, but to *believe* them. Most of us seek external validation – I know I sure as hell did – and when that approval and praise is not forthcoming, we start to doubt ourselves.

At this point in my preparations, my confidence was low, and validation was not forthcoming. My friends were calling me a loser because all I did was train and talk about the calorie-to-weight ratios of various freeze-dried meals. My boss was giving me sideways looks and glancing at his watch whenever I had to leave work slightly early for a gym session. I was out of the house regularly, and returning home sweaty and red-faced so often that my wife started to wonder if I was having an affair with the neighbour.

I did not have what you might call a hype team.

To be fair to my loving and supportive family, friends and colleagues, they were all giving me huge support, and cutting me a *lot* of slack from my various responsibilities to allow me to prepare for this race. That's why it hurt so much when I felt like I wasn't making any progress.

A reminder of this distinct lack of progress was delivered like a kick in the balls every single day because I had the good fortune to live atop a hill. I'd always seen this as positive thing in that I could sleep safely in the knowledge I would never wake up with floodwaters surging through my front door, and the kids could enjoy sledging on the one day every decade when a British winter delivered a decent covering of snow instead of rain. When I began running, however, I started to curse the day I'd chosen to live in a house situated on a 12% incline. No matter which running route I look, despite all the times I would open and reopen Google Maps, there was no avoiding it; I'd always have to finish my run with a slow, painful plod up a steep slope.

It was on a slightly warmer, marginally lighter morning in early March when I was trudging up that particular hill. As my 14-mile run was coming to an end, the loud house music blaring in my headphones was failing to drown out my self-dialogue, and on this day it appeared that I was stuck on shuffle between, *"Why aren't you in the pub with the rest of your friends?"* and *"You'll never be fit enough to do this race."*

I was so busy beating myself up that I didn't notice the unofficial markers that I had stopped at so many times. I ran past the postbox at the bottom of the hill against which, in previous months, I had collapsed with my head buried into the crook of my elbow, heaving for breath. I strode past the lamp post halfway up, against which I had leaned before to stop myself from passing out. As I reached the summit of my own miniature, personal Mount Everest, I carried on running past the street sign that still bore the faint stains of my vomit from when I had started my training. Before I knew it, I had reached the top. What's more, I didn't want to die.

Progress!

No one knew about this little victory but me. There was no medal, no cheering crowds and no photos. But, to me, this felt like an almighty achievement. This showed I was getting somewhere.

Since that day, I never underestimated the importance of progress. Whenever we embark upon a new physical or mental challenge, it is all too easy to get caught up in the big, exciting, scary goals. It's always so tempting to focus on where we want to get to that we ignore where we are starting from, but we must analyse and understand the point from which we begin in order to move forwards.

If you want to lose weight and get in shape, take pictures of yourself before you set foot in a gym for the first time. If you want to make a speech or go on stage, film your first terrifying, fumbling attempt. If you want to run, climb, row, cycle or swim, take a baseline measurement of your fitness and your initial wobbling, daunting, fumbling timings as you take the first faltering steps of your journey.

Technology makes it simple to track and measure our progress in whatever challenge we decide to undertake. In the dark days when it feels like we have gone nowhere at all, this can give us an invaluable boost of confidence to remind ourselves how far we have come. Technology, however, can also let our comfort zones pull us back in if we let it. So many training hours have been lost relaxing in the warm indoors waiting for a GPS signal. So many opportunities to improve have been wasted because a Fitbit or Garmin haven't been charged. It doesn't need to be expensive, and it doesn't need to be complicated. Before you leave the house and take that first step in training for a new challenge, take a look at a clock and note the time. When you get back, check the time again. Tomorrow, try to get back a minute quicker. That's all you need to do.

This is because whenever you finally complete whatever challenge you have set your heart on, it won't just be because of your performance on the day. The difference between success and failure in your journey will depend upon the small, tiny bits of progress you made along the way. It will be the accumulation of the tiny improvements – the seconds, minutes, inches and feet that will act as miniature signposts to tell you you're on the right path.

Then, one day, all those tiny steps of progress will lead you to victory.

*

This is why, on that second day out in the desert, when I was rudely awoken from my comforting dream to find myself having to run another marathon through one of the deadliest environments on the planet, I saw my choice. I knew I could choose to panic, to moan and to curse. I could make excuses, and blame the heat, the sand, the wind, my equipment, the race organisers or any other scapegoat I could point my dirty finger at.

Or I could accept my situation as a gift. I could remember the journey I had been on to get to this very patch of sand in one of the most beautiful places on earth. I could count my blessings to have somehow gathered the fitness and basic skills to be able to push myself forward against the odds. If all else failed, I'd just remind myself that I bloody volunteered for this race and paid for the damn thing, so the least I could do was put a smile on my face and enjoy it.

In the past, I would have limped and complained and allowed

my comfort zone to give me an excuse to quit. But, this time, I shut out the noise. I remembered the confidence and skills I had gathered throughout my long, painful training journey. There was no shouting, no bravado and no boastfulness. The moment was fleeting. All I did was gather my thoughts, and remind myself why I was doing this and how far I'd come. I gazed down at the golden folds of sand dancing and cascading over and around my feet like waves of an amber sea, and I decided to back myself.

As 'Highway to Hell' blasted over the loudspeakers once more, psyching the racers up to run a second marathon in as many days, I looked up and took one more step towards my conquer zone.

TEN

CONNECTING THE DOTS

As my legs buckled, my arse bounced off the jagged, grey rock with such force that it sent shockwaves of pain down to my toes. The only sounds I could hear were the rasping heaves of breath as I fought to suck air into my lungs. Lying flat on my back, with my arms flailing in the sand like a snow angel who had lost his way and found himself in hell, I squinted up at the cloudless, navy-blue sky.

Day three. We were definitely not on a beach holiday any more.

Like a stranded dung beetle, I managed to roll on to my stomach. With my arms stretched out in front of me and my chin embedded in the burning sand, I looked out across the barren desert plains and reflected upon the journey to get me to this point.

The third day had started as normal or, at least, as normal as you can get for someone who had been nursing a flat white and an iPad in the Gatwick Airport Starbucks six days earlier. The morning had begun with a rude dawn awakening as our pitiful shelter was dismantled around us while we were still shivering in our sleeping bags, trying desperately to regain a modicum of the body temperature the freezing desert night had stolen from us. Breakfast had consisted of porridge made from lukewarm water and eaten from a plastic bottle that been cut in half. Then it had been the morning trip to the toilets to do a poo in a plastic bag and piss on my shoes. Today had also been the day I decided to stop worrying about the cleanliness of my hands as I crouched down and struggled to insert contact lenses into my eyes, or to care about the small matter of not washing or changing my underwear for the last two days and 53 sand-filled miles.

For the time-being at least, I'd managed to dull the protests of my comfort zone that said everything I was doing was totally unnatural. I was trying to get comfortable with being uncomfortable.

As it turned out, 'comfortable being uncomfortable' sounds OK when you're sitting on a sofa watching a YouTube video on motivation or reading a book in a coffee shop. When you have just collapsed from heat exhaustion; the only thing hotter than the ground is the burning, relentless pain of lactic acid coursing through your legs; and a dehydration headache is pulverising your skull like a jackhammer – then it's not so enjoyable.

Lying on the sand, with my dry lips cracked and bleeding, I gazed with half-closed eyes at the alien landscape across which I'd just travelled. The day's running had started four hours earlier, and as the first thumping chords of 'Highway to Hell' carried across the fierce desert wind, I'd given my body a quick mental check: *pretty sore, very tired, feet hurt, could really do with a change of underwear, but otherwise OK.* Considering I'd never run two marathons in two days before and had certainly never attempted the feat in a place more dangerous than Liverpool on a Saturday night.

Moving forwards to the morning's start line with the crowd of nervous athletes, I had dug my race manual from my pocket. Every runner had been issued with one of these small journals before the race had started, and within it was contained a crudely hand-drawn map that detailed the challenges and tribulations we would encounter each day, along with the intimidating distances we needed to cover. Checkpoints were marked with a small box, and mountain ranges were distinguished by a collection of triangles, hugely underplaying their sheer size and scale. Dried riverbeds were shown as a set of thin, parallel lines flowing across the dusty and smeared pages. It was as if one of my children had been given some sheets of paper and a pencil, and then asked by a teacher to scribble the perfect landscape to really fuck Daddy up.

The sand dunes, however, were displayed using innocent-looking collections of thin waves, as if drawn by a delicate paintbrush. "A bit of sand," I muttered to myself as the day had begun and I broke into a jog, "Nothing wrong with a bit of sand. This morning will be a walk on a beach."

How wrong I was.

You know those really hot beach holidays you go on? When you're lying on a towel, and the warm can of gin and tonic has been drained, so you decided to go for a quick paddle in the sea. And then you step onto the sand and it feels like red-hot pokers have been shoved into your bare feet. So, you do that half-run-half-jump thing where you're trying to reach the cool relief of the water as quickly as possible while trying to minimise skin contact with the burning-hot ground? But you're a bit pissed, and it looks like you're trying to become a viral TikTok sensation by inventing a stupid new dance?

That is how hot the sand was. For ten miles.

I had reached the first dune and attacked it with fury, determined to not let it beat me. Surrounded by my companions, and with the sky filled with media helicopters buzzing low above our heads, the scene resembled a band of brothers going over the top of a trench in a distant, long-forgotten war. But, this time, the only enemy we faced was the desert itself.

After twenty metres of struggling, slipping and sliding against the constantly moving grains, which acted like a billion microscopic burning coals, I reached the peak triumphantly. I gave myself a small mental pat on the back and thought, *Maybe this won't be so bad after all.*

Then I saw what awaited me.

Sand stretched out as far as the eye could see. Dunes 10–20 metres high appeared to surge before me like waves across a stormy ocean. In front of me, golden, intimidating crests crashed against each other, the strong wind skimming a fine mist of dust from the peaks of the dunes to form a haze. This endless, intimidating ocean lay before me, with the amber shale fading to butterscotch, then lemon, and finally a dull grey-blonde in the distant heat haze that shimmered like a lake.

Steeling myself and setting my jaw in determination, I tried to ignore the fear and intimidation growing in my stomach, and I launched myself down the steep slope, trying to enter my conquer zone. My giant strides down the incline caused my legs to sink almost knee-deep in the burning sand, as if the desert itself was trying to capture and hold me there for eternity. At the base, I was welcomed by a small patch of hard, rocky ground, and thereafter the second dune awaited.

Nine miles later, I was on my arse. Literally. I collapsed at the base of a particularly evil-looking wall of sand and didn't believe I could go any further. The sucking, absorbing terrain had taken all my strength. My stomach growled with hunger, dehydration spun my head faster than any rollercoaster, and my lungs heaved as if I was in the 12th round of a heavyweight boxing match. What concerned me most of all, however, was the feeling of my mind breaking.

I was getting angry. Angry at the relentless sand, angry at myself for struggling up each peak and appearing to not be getting any closer to my goals, angry at the race organisers for devising such a fiendish route, and angry at the stupid bloody desert for being so fucking hot.

On attempting to rise, my legs screamed in protest. Running was long-forgotten now; I had lost the strength to charge *down* the steep slopes, let alone jog up them. As I struggled upwards on my hands and knees, the terrifying thought entered my head that I might fail in this challenge. With the door to my comfort zone left slightly ajar, dark thoughts and consequences rushed in like seawater through a holed ship's hull. I'd known this whole event would be the biggest physical challenge I'd ever faced, but now failure bore down upon me almost as strongly as the rising African sun.

Finally reaching the top of this latest monster, a faint object caught my eye: a signpost. It was embedded in the ground: firm, rocky, non-sandy ground. The end of this particular ordeal was in sight. I half-fell, half-rolled down the remaining dunes, no longer caring about the injuries I might sustain, or the extra helping of sand I'd serve into my eyes, mouth and ears.

Arriving in a heap at the bottom of that final dune, I could have cried with relief. My body protested and complained in pain, and a strange, moist rattling in my socks led to me to believe I'd lost a couple of toenails and gained a souvenir collection of raw, bleeding blisters in return.

Relief soon turned to confusion. I had been certain there would a checkpoint waiting for me after running the gauntlet of endless dunes for hours. The thoughts of momentary shade and four whole litres of pure, sweet, lukewarm water to quench my sandpapered throat and refill my dangerously low supplies had been the only beacon of hope that had kept me going through the last four hours. With dusty and bleeding fingers, I pulled out my race manual and checked the rudimentary map. The checkpoint should only be half a mile away, but I couldn't see it. Rechecking the map, I noticed a small, innocently drawn triangle nestling against the checkpoint marker. In slow motion, I looked at the page once more and then looked upwards. Facing me was a *jebel*; that is, a terrifying mountain of sand and rock that rose steeply out of the ground like a monolith, jutting almost vertically for a kilometre into the aquamarine sky. Looking closer, I could see what looked like ants scurrying across its surface. Then the realisation hit me: those ants were people, clinging on perilously as they struggled against time, heat and gravity – three things it would be unwise to pick a fight with at the best of times – to reach the distant summit.

The checkpoint certainly was half a mile away. Unfortunately, it was on the other side of this black and yellow elevation of death that was shaped like a hornet's arse.

I wanted to cry but was too dehydrated. All I knew was that I needed my conquer zone like never before. This was no longer about fitness, ability or stamina; any hint of athletic prowess had been long-abandoned in the sand. This was about trying to connect with

171

something deep inside my soul and using it to keep putting one foot in front of the other.

As I started my climb slowly, the sharp, black rocks jutted out of the sand like a dot-to-dot picture. My exhausted, shrivelled brain tried to connect a line between the dots and plot a course to the summit of this shifting, shimmering mountain. Staggering forwards, I eventually abandoned creating a strategy to reach my goal; it just felt like too much effort. Instead, I simply staggered upwards, trying to connect the dots between the rocks, searching meekly for the path of least resistance.

Stumbling ever higher, my legs started to wobble. I became distracted by the new, searing pain running down my back: my grimy t-shirt was caked in sand and grit, and my backpack was rubbing it against my skin, which was now covered in a layer of salt residue from my evaporated sweat. Working together in perfect, abrasive harmony, they rubbed the flesh on my spine away to a finish any carpenter would have been proud of.

Finally, when I could move forward no more, I toppled and fell. That rock I mentioned earlier tried its best to impale me through the arse, and I lay splayed on the sand like a spatchcocked chicken that had fallen off a beach barbecue. The desert mountain had won.

I raised my eyes to the heavens, asking if this was the time to raise the white flag. Air conditioning, a hot shower and a cold drink could be mine before too long. But as I gazed outwards, the forbidding landscape stretched out around me, reaching as wide as my hopelessness. The mountain had beaten me, and I didn't fancy a rematch anytime soon.

"*Monsieur, Monsieur!*" a voice called out.

I heard the soft, crunching sounds of feet running through sand. *A rescue party!* Someone must have spotted my plight and called for help, and now the medics had arrived to give me some much-needed hydration and help me off this peak.

The steps got closer and then stopped. I heard a faint clicking sound. *That must be the sound of the glass water bottles,* I told myself.

Admittedly, it did strike me as a little strange to be carrying heavy glass bottles. But, then again, on this day I'd already witnessed a woman bend over abruptly in front of me and do a poo, and a desert child had appeared from seemingly nowhere brandishing and offering to sell me what appeared to be world's most dangerous lizard. The only world he could say in English was 'PayPal'. So, at this point on this particularly soul-destroying day, a glass water bottle didn't seem particularly strange. All the same, I turned towards the sound.

Click. Click.

It wasn't the noise of a cool, clear bottle of water at all. It was the sound of a camera. One of the French media team had deemed my state of peril to be photo-worthy and had jumped out from behind a rock to fire off a couple of shots on their trusty Nikon as if I were a Z-list celebrity falling out of a nightclub.

I looked towards the man in a dazed state of disbelief.

"Dead! Dead, *Monsieur! Très bien,*" he shouted, and then showed me a thumbs up.

At least someone around here was having a good day out. Before he disappeared back behind the shaded safety of his rock, I called out in my best 'British man tries to order food in foreign country' voice.

"Oi, mate, is the checkpoint around here? Checkpoint? *Checkpoint!*"

Ignoring my communication skills, which wouldn't have been out of place in an episode of *Faulty Towers*, the man pointed to a cluster of specks in the distance. "*Oui.* You have arrived. Just 10 kilometres."

My head sank back into the sand. It was time to enter my conquer zone once more. On the bright side, it was all downhill from here.

*

By now, we all know that stepping into our conquer zone is a positive thing. It helps us achieve what we never thought we could be capable of. But to achieve true personal growth, and to hit those daunting, relentless, exciting goals we set ourselves, we need to keep going back into our conquer zones again and again. As we get ground down, tired and broken, the conquer zone seems less and less appealing. All of a sudden, we don't want to break down barriers and smash targets. We want to be in front of the TV, spilling ice cream on our pyjamas.

So when the going gets tough, how do we keep pushing ourselves into the conquer zone?

By connecting the dots.

When it comes to stepping out of your comfort zone, it helps to remember that everything is connected. I don't mean in a hippy, spiritual way (although I do believe this to be true, I'll leave the connected universe babble to the experts), but in different way.

Success isn't just about putting your head down and pushing yourself. It's about realising the tiny connections between your decisions, actions and behaviours that all add up to tip the scales in your favour – or put you at a massive disadvantage. Like a child completing a dot-to-dot picture, every time you connect another dot, that vision you want to achieve becomes more real. And this is how you do it:

1. ORGANISATION

It's not sexy, but it will help you connect the dots when you need it most. To give you an example, let's meet Frank. Frank was one of my tent buddies in the desert. I never discovered where he was from, what his job was or how old his kids were because, every time he spoke, he would say something like:

"Where's my fucking water bottle?"

"Who's moved my bastard sock?"

"I was literally just holding it in my sodding hand!"

"Has anyone used my toothbrush?"

You get the idea.

On the bright side, Frank was guaranteed to never get abandoned in the desert. A search party would recover him eventually by following the breadcrumb-like trail of water bottles, maps, emergency flares and venom pumps he would leave in his wake.

Needless to say, this lack of organisation caused his experience to be even more difficult and painful than it needed to be. You can't step into your conquer zone if you're too busy looking for your shoe.

When the journey towards achieving your goals gets rocky, as mine certainly did, you need to be able to focus on the task at hand. When the going got tough, and I had to climb the world's biggest sandcastle, I needed to use every ounce of energy and focus on simply not giving up. Now, I will be first to admit I'm not the most organised person in the world, but taking a bit of time before your challenge to work out what you need, where it needs to be and how you need to use it can make all the difference.

Plus, when it comes to being organised, it isn't just about the big and obvious things, such as bags, passports, maps, underwear and insulin. It's the small stuff. If anything, the tiny details are more likely to fuck up your trip to the conquer zone because you won't realise they matter until it's too late. On this day when the Saharan Desert sand almost wiped me out, it wasn't my fitness that got me through, it was the fact I was (just about) organised. The big things mattered – I'd picked decent shoes, managed to not run out of water and decided to wear a hat – and they would certainly have turned a bad day into a terrible one had I got them wrong. However, it was the small details that were vital: taking a tiny salt tablet religiously every 30 minutes, understanding how to read a basic map and having the discipline to not devour all the food in my backpack, like a child on a school excursion. If I had got just *one* of the of the finer points wrong, it would have been the end of my race.

Being organised when it comes to the big and small details doesn't just apply to stupid endurance races. It will help you overcome whatever challenge you are undertaking:

- Giving a speech at a wedding? What pocket of your outfit will your script go in? Doing the panicked pat-down as if your best shirt has suddenly ignited is not the way to calm the nerves when you're stepping up to the stage and can't find your paperwork.

- Want to take that adventure abroad? What will the climate be like? What advice do other people give on the area? Do you need vaccinations? Are there local scams that get pulled on unsuspecting, disorientated tourists as they step out of the airport?

Some of this stuff might not be cool, and I might be running the risk of sounding like your mum, but it works. Understand the small items that will help you reach your goals, and make sure you know how you're going to use them. In a way, *how* you do it doesn't really matter (unless we're talking about a defibrillator or venom pump, you might want to swot up on things like that), but what does matter is that it works for *you* with *consistency.*

But how do you know what you need to organise? There's a little trick for that…

2. VISUALISATION

Visualisation isn't just the stuff of elite athletes staring down a 100-metre racetrack, or gurus sitting cross-legged in their cushion-covered sanctuaries. It can help all of us.

The common perception of visualisation is that it is used to achieve success. *Picture yourself achieving your goal and it will happen,* etc. That's all very well and good, and – for what it's worth – I've used visualisation in this way plenty of times. Sometimes it's worked, such as when I visualised myself at the Marathon des Sables start line, but other times the results haven't been quite as forthcoming, such as when I spent most of my teenage years imagining that Pamela Anderson would appear magically in my bedroom. I guess sometimes even the universe can't deliver.

Visualisation can help us achieve our goals, not just through imagining what the end result would be like but also what the journey will be to get there. In this case, visualisation helps us run through tens if not hundreds of what-if scenarios in our heads to help us be prepared as possible. Give this a try:

1. Sit or lie in a location where you won't be interrupted. An empty house (preferably your own): good. A local soft-play centre when it's Haribo happy hour: bad.

2. Take a few slow, deep breaths in through the nose and out through the mouth, and imagine you're in an audience watching a TV show. The show features you, executing perfectly whatever it is you want to achieve (this is called the 'distant image'). See as much detail as you can: the location, the weather, the time of day, who else is with you, what they are wearing and what they are saying. Pay attention carefully to what you are thinking, feeling and doing.

3. Now (in your mind, remember) step into the TV show. You're no longer watching yourself undertaking this challenge, but you're living it through your own eyes (this is called the 'embodied image'). It will make the whole experience feel more vivid and allow you to connect more deeply with what is happening all around you, the successes you're achieving – and the challenges you're overcoming.

4. At this point, you're in the middle of your very own virtual conquer zone. But this isn't about congratulating yourself prematurely for hitting another goal, it's about running through scenarios. Think of it as stepping into a mental simulator where you can test things out and try them in your mind before you have to go through them for real.

Let's work through an example. Before heading out to the desert, I would spend hours visualising and walking through different scenarios (this is when my family thought I'd finally lost the plot). Sure, I couldn't *exactly* understand what the desert would be like or know how I'd react in those conditions, but I could visualise how I would react if one of these happened:

- I got lost
- My shoes broke

- My water bottles started leaking
- I got stung by a scorpion
- I contracted diarrhoea and shit in my only pair of pants
- I was told of a family emergency at home
- My contact lenses got lost or my sunglasses got broken
- My map blew away
- I got bitten by a camel
- I got bitten by a camel spider
- My toenails fell off
- A tornado hit my tent and blew all my possessions away
- I got caught in a sandstorm in the middle of the night and had to survive in the desert alone until sunrise

I know some of these situations sound unlikely and others downright crazy. Except they aren't. Each of the above circumstances actually happened to someone during my race. The people who were organised and were able to adapt stepped into their conquer zones and carried on. Those who were haphazard, disorganised and taking a punt on the whole thing often found their race was over. When those competitors were watching the finishers receive their medals, they often blamed circumstances, bad luck or other people.

What they did not realise was that when we step out of our comfort zones, shit is *going* to go wrong. Rather than blame everyone and everything, we need to step up, take responsibility, visualise our journeys and get prepared.

I know it all sounds a little bit hippy. But those bohemian flower children over at NASA and the military special forces use these techniques a lot to practice for every eventuality before setting off on a mission. Getting visualised means getting organised. It's much better to build confidence and know you're prepared for every eventuality. The alternative (and we've all done this) is to rock up to a meeting/ presentation/challenge/race/date knowing deep down that we've not prepared, done our homework or got organised. Then we just have to sit and hope, with the feeling of panic inside, praying nothing goes wrong and wishing we'd just stayed inside our comfort zones in the first place.

Of course, this all sounds good in theory. We all know that being organised is generally better than being disorganised, and it's always preferable to have a plan, but everyone has a plan until they poo their pants. Unexpected things sometimes happen. Anyone who has a tidied a house before a child walks in knows that nothing stays organised forever.

In the next section we'll look at what happens when things go *really* wrong (and believe me, they do), but when stuff doesn't go quite as you expect, it's important to remember…

3. THERE IS MORE THAN ONE WAY TO WIN

It's fair to say that – despite my best intentions, and all the organisation, visualisation, lists, Post-its and preparation, day three of my race was not my finest hour. The desert was well and truly bending me over and giving me a whipping. And not in a good way.

But did this mean I had lost? Far from it. If anything, these tribulations would make my victory sweeter, but I'd need to be in my conquer zone mindset to truly enjoy the success.

But what is success? To step away from our comfort zones fully, we need to understand what success means to us for a particular challenge or adventure. I had to understand if success for me was *winning* the world's toughest footrace, meaning I would be forever chasing the impossible. If, however, success was knowing I had overcome every challenge the race had presented to me, given every ounce of my strength and left absolutely nothing out on that sandy field, then victory was still possible.

It's dangerous to embark on any kind of challenge or adventure believing that everything is going to go your way and you'll basking in the glory of cheering crowds when you finish. There's only one way you get that kind of happy ending every time: by staying in your comfort zone, taking it easy and never pushing yourself to see what might happen. To understand what you are truly capable of, you must stare failure in the face.

We tend to think of success in black-and-white terms: win or lose; pass or fail, and triumph or defeat. It doesn't have to be like this. It is more effective (and more realistic) to think of it as a spectrum with the perfect outcome at one end and absolute disaster at the other. Generally, the results of whatever we achieve sit either towards one point or the other, but success rarely happens through everything going perfectly, nor does absolute failure occur similarly.

There is more than one way to conquer our goals. In order to understand this, I used the Podium Method. The Podium Method recognises that, if you are standing on the podium, then you are victorious. This isn't in a fluffy, 10th-place-trophy, special-snowflake kind of way. This is an approach for those who are truly willing to go into their conquer zones, try something new and push themselves to their absolute limits. And the best part is that it rewards those who are prepared to take *any* kind of step out of their comfort zones.

A binary, *win-or-lose* approach only gives you one chance of success. Quite simply, you are either successful or you aren't. The Podium Method gives you not one, not two, but *three* shots at being successful at everything you try.

The technique is simple. When you are preparing for a challenge, when you are visualising that goal, you want to identify three different levels of outcome. Just like a podium at the Olympics, you want to establish your gold, silver and bronze results.

Gold is the absolute best outcome you can hope for. In the Marathon des Sables, for me, this was finishing in the top 100 places. My silver outcome was to finish in the top half of the competitors. The bronze outcome? Just to finish the race.

Three different outcomes and three different victories, but each one of them would still be a success. I could easily have started the race saying to myself, "My goal is to finish in the top 100 and nothing else will make me happy." However, as my race went on, if that goal became even more distant, I would have become despondent. With my desired outcome being more and more unlikely, my mood would have got darker and that whispering comfort zone would have got louder.

But when my goal of finishing in the top 100 wasn't going to happen (if the many people running past me while I was collapsed in the sand was anything to go by), I was able to deal with it because I knew I still had my silver outcome to aim for: finish in the top half of the field.

Even if my race had started to disintegrate and I had fallen further down the rankings, I'd still be able to focus on my bronze goal of just crossing the finishing line. These three different types of victory allowed me to adapt my focus as my race and fortunes changed, while always giving me something to aim for.

Why not just set myself the goal of crossing the finish line, you may ask? I could have done this, but setting ourselves a target of just doing the bare minimum is never conducive to stepping into our conquer zones. If I had aimed to compete, not complete, that joy of crossing the finish line could have been soured with a nagging question of doubt from my comfort zone asking, "Could you have done more?"

Finally, even if you mess up and fail to hit even your bronze target, you will still learn and gain experience. Is it really a failure? Even the people who didn't finish their race discovered something about themselves.

So, to connect the dots, it's all about organisation, visualisation and understanding that there is more than one way to win. If you can do these three things, then you can give yourself the best chance of success when facing setback after setback and staring adversity in the face.

Just remember, if you're still breathing, you're still winning.

*

I staggered into camp at the end of day three, collected my water ration and collapsed in a heap on the holed and pungent blanket that was to be my mattress for the night. Ignoring the stones digging into my arse, I reflected on a day in which I had been truly pushed to my limits. My stomach cramped and flipped somersaults, informing me

I'd burned in the region of 6,000 calories for the third day in a row. Also, for the third consecutive day, I'd only taken 2,500 calories back on board. I'm not a nutritionist (nor a mathematician for that matter), but those numbers weren't good. I was losing weight faster than a socialite who had adopted a cocaine-based diet.

Race rules stipulated that each competitor had to have a minimum of 2,000 calories per day. Having to carry all our food on our backs had meant I'd taken a risk on going low on calories in order to keep my pack weight down and move faster through the desert. Now I was in the race, however, I was starting to have my doubts. I was light on calories but not light on my feet. I could only hope a solid foundation built up from years of Guinness, pies, chocolate and pizza would see me through to the finish line.

As the sun's final bronze and gilded rays lengthened the shadows of the 100 black tents of the camp, a few figures staggered towards a large fire in the centre of the settlement. As they huddled together and talked in soft murmurs, the atmosphere felt charged with anticipation. The scene could have taken place 1,000 years ago: troops killing time nervously, with their senses on edge and unable to sleep, fully alert in the knowledge that war would come at dawn.

And war was indeed on its way. Despite all the mishaps, knockdowns and predicaments we had faced so far, we were all too well aware that the greatest battle against ourselves was about to commence. For tomorrow was the dreaded 'long day', a non-stop, 56-mile charge across the desert that had to be completed within 36 hours. I was about to learn that everything I had experienced so far would pale in comparison to the challenges I was about to face.

ELEVEN

DARKNESS

"Have you ever seen anything so beautiful?"

Such tender words sounded strange when pronounced in Cameron's deep, Welsh-valleys accent. The heaviness of his voice boomed across the empty desert, making me jump. I had been too preoccupied with rearranging my underwear and shorts with fumbling, frozen fingers to notice his arrival. The piss I'd just taken had been the same as the one 10 minutes ago and the one 10 minutes before that: bright pink with blood.

"All OK with you, boyo?" my new companion asked.

"Yep, fine," I lied. "It's amazing how water goes right through you when it's rationed."

Cameron's eyes shone in the pitch-black – two gleaming specks almost as bright as the billions of stars in the cloudless sky above us. He looked upwards once more, and this time I followed his gaze. He was right; it was one of the most majestic sights I had ever witnessed.

The swirling patterns of the Milky Way began from a hidden horizon somewhere on my left, stretched into the heavens, over my head, and disappeared into some invisible mountain range on my right. It was if all the diamonds in the world had been scattered across a deep, inky-black, velvet rug and illumined for my eyes only.

In that enchantingly black sky, the only movements that caught my eye were the brilliant, burning, urgent darts of shooting stars blazing through the atmosphere, and the straight, calm, relentless monotony of satellites and the International Space Station charting a straight line across the darkness.

The beauty of it all was such that it distracted me from my predicament for a few moments. Then, as the blinding pain shot from the top of my neck down to my kidneys once more, I remembered my situation.

Not for the first time, I was in a hell of a state.

*

The 'long day' had started with a mixture of bravado and misplaced confidence. I had somehow picked myself back up from the misfortunes on the world's biggest mountain of sand, and I was feeling surprisingly positive. I was ready to step into my conquer zone, and the prospect of a double marathon somehow seemed manageable. Even though I'd never run more than 26 miles in a day before, I was ready for anything.

As 'Highway to Hell' once again filled my eardrums, I prepared to throw my body and mind into my conquer zone once more. A total of 56 miles or 90 kilometres: that was the distance between me and the end of the stage. Those kinds of numbers were almost *too* big to be intimidating. Similar to when someone announces you owe them £1 billion, and you laugh because the sheer scale of the number is too large to be taken seriously. But I knew this was serious; I'd never even thought about attempting to move this kind of distance before without four wheels underneath me.

"Break it down," I told myself. "Just think of it as running a 10k race. Nine times. Or just doing 18 parkruns." No matter which way I'd spun it in my mind, I hadn't been able to get my head around the challenge I faced.

Days four and five were about to become the toughest of my life.

The morning had started suspiciously easily. This proved once again what a wonder the human body and mind is at adapting to hostile and uncomfortable situations. By this fourth day of my challenge, I was getting more and more familiar with my conquer zone, and I could feel myself growing in confidence and challenging myself every day.

As the sun travelled across the cloudless sky, I shuffled through wide salt plains that had been humid lakebeds back in a long-forgotten time, but that were now baked solid by the relentless desert heat. I struggled up giant hills of jagged rocks, and across miles of deep, energy-sapping sand dunes that tried to pull me backwards with every step.

When the sun edged closer to the horizon, casting deep orange, purple and maroon hues across a slate-grey sky, I reached a checkpoint and started to run through my usual routine. I drank all the remaining water in the two bottles strapped to my chest, and then accepted two new 2-litre bottles from the race marshals. With one of the bottles, I refilled my own water supply. I downed as much of the second bottle as I possibly could, as if I were a rugby player in a drinking contest, and poured the remaining contents over my head. Taking a second to collect myself, I perched on the least-sharp rock I could find, and cradled my head in my arms to catch my breath and moment's respite. I checked my watch: I'd been moving non-stop through the desert for 10 hours.

One of the race organisers approached me. "Chin up, mate; you're almost halfway."

Great. One marathon down, only another to go.

I hauled my sore arse off its perch and staggered onwards as the sun dipped below the horizon. Darkness fell rapidly across the desert as I turned on my headtorch, snapped my glowstick and attached it to my backpack. I took a breath and stepped into the gloom. Nightfall in the Sahara Desert was like flicking a switch. It felt like a scorching oven had transformed instantaneously into a silent, cold ecosystem, and I was stuck in a place that was simply, well, nothing.

I soon lost all concept of time and distance.

The world around me had shrunk: my entire existence was reduced to the few metres of light cast by my feeble headtorch as my head swayed nervously from side to side. The majestic grandeur of the desert had been diminished to oblivion. Marching forwards, the only clue I had as to my surroundings was the terrain beneath my feet. I had no idea if I were about to enter a vast collection of sand dunes or commence a journey across vast salt plain as smooth as a sheet of steel.

The only indications that I was not about to walk off the edge of a cliff were the tiny pinpricks of light bobbing in front of me. The faint glimmers from the glowsticks attached to the competitors miles ahead of me provided a vague waypoint, so I fixed my eyes on these mini balls of light, and I strode forwards.

At first, everything was under control. Alone in the desert, my mind switched between a state of high alert – my senses alive and on-edge for the slightest sound or movement in the darkness – and a deeper, more meditative state of consciousness. Abstract swarms of thoughts glided through my mind, ranging from the insignificant (*Why is sand yellow?*) to the soul-searching (*Am I happy with how I have lived my life so far?*). My thoughts flipped inwards, outwards and back to front, as I dwelled on everything and nothing.

My body became a monotonous machine; trudging forwards, with my arms swinging for momentum, my only other movement would be to take a sip of water religiously every 10 minutes, and pop in another salt tablet every 30 minutes. Despite the furnace-like temperatures of the desert plummeting to just above freezing in 90 minutes, my body was still sweating. Throughout this adventure, I had been able to top up the gallons of fluid I was losing through sweat by drinking water. But in order to replace the salts and minerals we were also shedding, all competitors had been given a party pack of salt tablets before the race. These would keep our electrolytes balanced and our bodies in working order. Too few tablets would cause us to start to experience nausea, cramps and vomiting, which would eventually lead to collapse and kidney shutdown. Too many tablets would lead us to suffer extreme thirst (never a good thing in a desert), fatigue, confusion, dangerously high blood pressure and potential kidney shutdown.

Either way, it didn't sound like a good day out for my kidneys.

I hadn't paid too much attention to the medical briefing six days earlier, which felt like a different lifetime ago. I remember something about "X number of tablets combined with Y litres of water every Z hours," but found my mind tripping over itself. That's dyslexia for you.

Instead I'd taken the advice from one of the veteran runners: "Pop one of those in your gob every 30 mins, like you're in Ibiza and chomping on Ecstasy pills. If it feels like someone has stabbed you in the kidney, then take another for good luck."

That sounded good enough for me.

On I went, warily, through the darkness. Stride. Sip. Swallow.

Then the wind began.

The storm didn't creep up like a thief in the night, it attacked with the force of a detonation. The gale punched me hard, and then delivered a high-pressure blast of sand into my eyes and mouth as a follow up. I pulled my neck scarf around my face and tried to shrink my head into my shoulders, making myself as small as possible so as to not expose myself to the onslaught of wind and dust.

I continued forwards into the vortex, my half-closed eyes searching for the tiny glowsticks ahead to mark my route.

There were none.

My vision was obscured by a blizzard of sand, dust and grit spinning around me like a banshee. Now all I could rely on were the faint divots and footprints in the sand, illuminated by my headtorch. For the first time, a strangled yelp of panic threatened to escape my throat. Fear was upon me.

I swallowed and noticed that my tongue was stuck to the roof of my mouth with the kind of acrid dryness I used to remember from when I'd wake face down on the sofa on a Sunday morning, surrounded by empty cans and wine bottles.

"Don't panic. Breathe. Focus. Think." I stopped for a moment, turned my back to the roaring wind, and took a big sip of water. Then another. Then another long drink. It was too much liquid.

"Nothing out here wants to hurt you," I tried to remind myself. *"The biggest threat to your success is your mind."*

Disorientated in the turmoil, I started to become disorganised. Undone shoelaces trailed in my wake, I gulped water when thirsty, but my salt-tablet supply was left untouched. *"Just keep going,"* I told myself, even though I had lost sight of my goal.

After what felt like hours of staggering through relentless winds and sandblasting, a faint glow appeared ahead. At first, I thought my eyes were playing tricks, which was a side effect of having sand thrown into them continuously. Yet the faint light grew and grew, until I could make out a collection of lamps, and the stronger beams of a Land Rover's headlights reaching out to me like two welcoming arms.

A checkpoint!

As I staggered into the tiny collection of tents, two 2-litre bottles of water were shoved into my arms. I repeated my usual drill: drink, refill, drink as much as you can, and refill. This time, however, there was no chance of pouring a bottle over my head – I had begun to shiver violently as soon as I stopped moving.

Taking a moment to crouch down and gather my strength, I looked at the scene around me. The checkpoint resembled a makeshift army base in the front line of some distant desert war. Bodies were strewn everywhere: people were splayed face down in the dirt trying to snatch a few moments' sleep, sitting on backpacks with their heads in their hands, or lying on low camp beds with the thin, translucent wire of an intravenous drip snaking into their arms. It was impossible to move without kicking discarded water bottles, blood- and pus-stained bandages, and empty energy-gel wrappers.

The desert was taking no prisoners, and the body count was growing by the minute.

I shook my head to clear the dizziness and tried to force fluid down myself until I retched like a water-boarded prisoner. Still, the pounding headache refused to shift. *On the bright side,* I told myself, *at least it was distracting me from the growing pain in my kidneys.*

The desire to fall to the floor and sleep had never been greater. I craved comfort. Lying in the dirt and curling into a ball appealed to me as much as the Presidential Suite at the Savoy. The clock had just passed midnight: I had been moving non-stop for almost 18 hours, and there was still over 10 miles to go.

My comfort zone gave me 100 reasons to quit: "*You need rest and you need fuel; sit down and check your feet; lie down and get some sleep; your body needs time to recover; just wait until the sun comes and move again in daylight.*" In fairness to that troublesome part of my brain that had kept me safe, warm, bored and unfulfilled for so long – it was absolutely right.

It didn't help that my conquer zone could provide only one argument in response: "*Don't you want to see what you are truly capable of?*"

"For *fuck's* sake," I muttered as I secured my drinks bottles and tightened the straps on my backpack. It was now or never. And, deep down, I knew that if I stopped at this moment, then it might well be never.

As if finally having sympathy for my plight, the desert storm ended as abruptly as it had started. The wild wind scampered away across the pitch-black dunes, and the violent clouds of sand retreated, leaving only a cascade of stars suspended above my head. As I trudged forward, I gave a half-smile, half grimace – that view was enough to take the pain away for a few seconds at least. The peace was shattered suddenly by a booming sound at my side that made me jump two feet in the air.

"You look like you could use some company, my lad."

And before I could protest or say otherwise, Cameron was in my life.

*

Many words could be used to describe Cameron, but 'discreet' would not be one of them. His booming voice announced the arrival of a six-foot-six-inch giant carved from slate, looming straight out of the Welsh valleys. If you were to picture the absolute antithesis of a long-distance ultrarunner, it would be Cameron. He was neither slight nor wiry nor lithe – his barrel chest was straining against the seams of the bright-red jacket he wore to protect himself from the freezing desert night. Propelling himself forward with mighty strides, he was easily able to keep pace with my miniature, pitter-patter footsteps as I performed the impossible feat of running slower than another man could walk. The majority of Cameron's face was covered in an unkempt, black beard, but the covering of wiry hair failed to conceal a beaming smile and eyes that shone with friendliness and support, almost as brightly as the stars. A hand-knitted, red-and-white hat emblazoned with the Welsh dragon – or it could have been a cat – sat atop his head, with the furry bobble swaying gently as he moved his head to speak to me. "Caught sight of you at that last checkpoint, I did. Thought you looked in a hell of a state. Couldn't believe my eyes when you decided to keep going, like."

I gave him a glance and a half-smile. "Well, the finish line isn't getting closer, so we might as well get this over with."

"Right you are, lad," came the solid response, "Well, let's get through this little trot together then, shall we?"

It was meant as a question, but something told me I didn't have a say in the matter. I was stuck with Cameron for the foreseeable future.

I'd always considered myself an awkward mix of introvert and extrovert. I enjoyed the company of others, but my social circle had always been small. Growing up an only child, I'd often dreamed about being the popular kid at school, then the life and soul of the party when I was older. I wanted to be that guy who entered a bar to a loud cheer, or the employee who would walk into a networking event and strike up a conversation with anyone, then leave with a roomful of newly inspired business contacts and associates. But, for me, it was not to be. I had focused naturally on the quality, not quantity of friends.

I tended to nurture deep friendships for life, rather than skim across hundreds of superficial relationships. But, instead of accepting who I was, I chose to beat myself up. I had spent years telling myself that I was doing something 'wrong' by not being popular enough, being charming enough, being outgoing enough or networking enough. While I knew that I was never going to make my dreams come true by hiding in my comfort zone, I fell into a trap of thinking being popular was 'right' and being satisfied in my own company was 'wrong'. But, despite hating myself for it, I still couldn't change who I was.

This is why I found it so difficult when Cameron took a size-12 step into my life and refused to leave. Shattering my self-constructed prison of solitude, he entered my consciousness and intruded into my thoughts. Like it or not, I was stuck with him.

It's not so bad, I told myself. At least talking to Cameron made the minutes and footsteps pass quicker, and took my mind off the stabbing pains in the small of my back. We spoke of our lives, our families, our hopes, our dreams, and our reasons for throwing ourselves so far out of our comfort zones and spending a week of our lives charging through this cursed desert. It transpired that he had a similar background to me – slightly older and higher up the corporate ladder – but, essentially, he'd entered the race for the same reason I had: to prove to himself and his children that anyone could achieve anything they set their minds to.

Despite my initial misgivings, I couldn't help but warm to his broad Welsh accent and a laugh that echoed across the empty sands like a foghorn. Whenever I winced in pain or gave one of those exasperated gasps when your lungs empty themselves as if throwing their contents down in surrender, he found the words of support I needed, be it the quietly encouraging, "Come on now, buddy; I know you've got this. Dig deep now," or the rather less friendly, "Move your fucking legs, you English twat. You're a fucking disgrace to your family, and your dead relatives would be ashamed to see you piss your pants in this fucking desert. Move your arse!"

It was very much a carrot-or-stick approach. But whether

Cameron's words brought me to the edge of laugher or tears, he always managed to say the right thing to keep me putting one front in front of the other.

Cameron even kindly waited for me when I started to need the toilet. Every ten minutes I would apologise, stop, take a piss, then carry on. It was only after the fifth or sixth occurrence that an alarm triggered in my fractured and tired brain: *something's wrong.*

When I once again felt the call of nature, I shone my torch downwards to see what was happening. Scorpions darted for cover as the beam of light hit the ground, their tiny legs creating a criss-cross pattern of pinpricks as they scampered across the sand. On any other day, the sight of real, live, stinging scorpions would have been a cause for greater concern. But it appeared I had bigger things to worry about.

My urine shone bright pink in the torchlight. I was pissing blood. The shock discovery snapped my foggy mind into perfect clarity. I started to put clues together: the constant thirst, the pain in the small of my back, getting sloppy with my salt tablets, needing the toilet every 10 minutes, and not to mention wee the colour of cranberry juice. I jumped to conclusions faster than a hypochondriac using Google: *kidney failure.*

The colour must have drained from my face, causing it to glow a ghostly pale in the moonlight, because Cameron had stopped smiling finally. "What's up, boyo? A snake hasn't bitten you on the dick, has it?"

This would have been the perfect moment to ask for help, share my worrying discovery and create a plan for rescue with my new companion. But, like most other men, I did none of these things. "No, it's all good, mate. Just getting tired of having to stop and piss every two minutes."

"Right you are then. Shall we crack on?"

I gave a small nod, stepped once more into the darkness and commenced the most terrifying hours of my life.

Failing this challenge had always been something I was aware of but had never really acknowledged. Whenever a friend or loved one had mentioned the possibility of not reaching the finish line, I had reacted with anger and arrogance. "*Why don't you believe in me? I can achieve anything I want!*" I would yell like a spoiled child who considered success to be pretty much guaranteed rather than earned. But as I staggered through the pitch blackness, my desire for success had been replaced by a greater need: survival.

Outwardly, I was silent, my face a stony mask of determination. But I was panicking inside: "*How long to the finish line? Do I stop drinking water to give my kidneys a break? Will that make me more dehydrated? When did I last take a salt tablet? How long will it take for help to get here? Should I raise the alarm?*" Thoughts as dark as the night sky raced through my head at an increasing rate, like a snowball of negativity rolling down a mountain.

As if sensing my distress, Cameron paused, threw his head towards the heavens and turned off his headtorch. "Have you ever seen anything so beautiful?"

And this brings us back to the beginning of the end.

*

I had never truly contemplated death before. It was always there in the background, as an inevitability I knew I would face eventually. But, at the same time, I never really paid it much attention. Death was something that happened to other people – my father included – and I knew I could use it as an excuse to live *in* fear, to live *without* fear or to live in *denial*.

As I walked through the desert, tripping and stumbling over rocks and divots, no longer seeing nor caring where I was placing my feet, I pondered whether I had pushed my conquer zone too far this time.

As I stopped to piss blood yet again – with my body swaying like a drunk, and my vision clouding – I vaguely considered the irony of my predicament. The death of my father had caused me to take a long, hard look at my safe, gluttonous life and ask myself if this was how it was going to be for the rest of my days. I had forced myself to leave comfort's shadow and move into my conquer zone in order to experience more, to give more and to live more. Yet here I was, supposedly stepping into a brave, new way of living and a bold, new way of *being* – and if I wasn't careful, it was going to get me killed.

The stars above twinkled and glimmered as if taunting me silently from distant worlds: *Why did you ever think you were good enough?*

I contemplated my fate and realised the outcomes were not looking great. I'd suffered for too long and help in the darkness was too far away. For the first time in my life, I tried to accept that death was upon me. It's often said a strange, inevitable calm descends upon those who understand that death is near. I can only claim the feeling is one of annoyance. I thought of my sons and was angry at putting myself in a position where I might not see them grow up. I was disappointed that I had not been a better, more attentive husband. And, finally, I was hugely pissed off that an attempt to leave my comfort zone and make my dreams come true was going to result in my spectacular, fatal failure.

"*You should have just been happy with your average life,*" my comfort zone scolded me. "*You're nothing different. Nothing special. Why were you stupid enough to try to be something you weren't? You could have enjoyed a long, normal, uneventful life. And now you've blown it.*"

I sank to my knees, my hands clasped to my back as I yelped in pain, broken by the realisation that I had failed. I'd failed the race, failed my family and failed myself. And now it could cost me my life. For the first time, I truly gave up all hope and let the darkness win.

"Who told you to stop there, lad?" came the voice. "You're not finished yet."

I opened one eye to see Cameron standing above me. How embarrassing. "I am finished," I replied. "I'm ruined. I've failed. It's over for me. It's all fucked. Totally fucked." I leaned forwards and ground my fists into the dirt in frustration.

"No one is saying that apart from you, though," Cameron

countered calmly in his deep, slow voice. He continued, "I'm not saying those words. No one else is here to tell you that story. The only person who believes you're finished is *you*."

"*It's over. I've failed!*" I shouted up at him between clenched teeth.

"You're not a fucking failure," he retorted. "If you were a failure, you'd be on that sofa at home, telling everyone how you were going to run through the desert one day, but then you wouldn't do it. You'd just sit on your arse, make excuses, bitch and moan, and say you'd be making your dreams happen if it wasn't for money or time or work." Cameron fired his words at me like bullets from a machine gun, his finger stabbing repeatedly in my direction to emphasise his point.

I had to admit, I was impressed that he had enough energy for such an animated performance.

Before I could answer, he fired another volley. "Why are you so bloody scared of failure anyway? You're so fucking stupid. I've heard your story: for so long you didn't try because you were scared to fail. But don't you *see*? The only way you fail is if you *don't* try. Never stepping out of your comfort zone makes you a failure. By trying something different, by attempting something you've never done before, it's *impossible* to be a total failure!"

It almost brought a tear my eye, or would have if I'd had any moisture left in my body.

"I still can't carry on, mate. I think I'm dying."

"Bullshit! You haven't come this far to only come this far!"

As his words sunk in, I thought of my father and what he would say if he were with me. Then I realised he'd probably tell me to just give up and find a pub. But I also knew that, even though he wasn't one of those fathers who would hug me, take me to the football or particularly care about my children, he would silently have been proud that his son got off his arse and stopped making excuses for not living the life he dreamed of.

My mind was transported back to the distant past, when I was sitting on a threadbare sofa in a cloud of smoke so thick it caused my asthma to clench my chest like a vice, making me pull and heave to suck enough oxygen into my lungs. My father was staring out of the lounge window, a stained wineglass in one hand and a cigarette with an inch of ash dangling precariously from it in the other. I did not know what answers he was looking for in the darkness, but his words were forever stamped into my soul: "Don't let anything beat you down, Freddie. No person, situation or circumstance can define who you are. You have the world in front of you, but you have to decide whether to control it or to let it control you. This stupid fucking life is not a fairy tale, but you can write your own story, and you can change the world."

I'd only asked him if we could go to the park tomorrow.

Back from my abstracted memories, collapsed on my knees in the middle of the wilderness, I knew I had a choice that would define my future. I could give up – on the race, on my life and on my future – or I could pick myself up and carry on. At that moment, I didn't know if I could change the world, but I knew I could change *my* world.

Cameron was right. With a growl that sounded suspiciously like a wail, I half-rolled, half-staggered to my feet.

My race was back on.

Little was said between Cameron and me in that final hour of the night, although I felt his eyes upon me constantly, ready to support me if I stumbled or faltered. Plenty, however, was said between me and my father. Silently, I asked him so many questions, and I pleaded for the answers and reasons behind so many of the things he'd said and done in the past. Although the heavens gave me no response, in my soul, he and I created the peace and understanding I'd always craved.

A flash of light accompanied by a dull, monotonous, mechanical sound snapped me from my distant thoughts and memories. A faint, minty aroma filled my nostrils, with the clean freshness of the scent as alien as the landscape I had just dragged myself though.

"Fix up and look sharp, my lad," Cameron murmured, "You've made it."

Through tear-filled eyes I saw the shining lights of the camp, beckoning me into its sanctuary. The cheers of the watching race marshals and the gathered elite racers who had finished hours earlier drowned out the hum from the power generators. Flashbulbs from media crew made me flinch and turn, not just because my eyes had become too accustomed to the darkness, but because my existence had become so unfamiliar with success.

Cameron stepped into the shadows and motioned with his hand for me to continue forwards. "You go and enjoy this, boyo; you've earned it tonight."

As I staggered across the marker line, my electronic tracking tag released a small, joyous beep of victory marking the end of the 56-mile stage. I collapsed to the floor in a delirious state of uncontrolled laugher mixed with unstoppable tears. Marshals ran to help me to my feet and passed me a paper cup of steaming mint tea. I accepted it with shaking hands and smiled as I savoured the warm, sweet taste.

My time in the darkness was over.

*

The struggles I encountered that night brought me closer than ever to death, and taught me more about my life than I could ever have imagined. I learned more through staring failure in the face than I ever could have by staying comfortable and enjoying easy success. But the prospect of failure, as I also discovered, was a by-product of fully embracing my conquer zone. What I learned from myself – and from Cameron – that night could be used by anyone, in any situation when the going gets tough and defeat is a more likely outcome than victory. Four things – momentum, foolishness, support and faith – are the strategies you can employ at that moment when entering your own conquer zone feels like the worst decision you ever made.

1. MOMENTUM

When would you rather be standing in front of a train ('never' is the obvious but unacceptable answer here): when it is pulling away slowly from a platform or under full speed 10 miles down the track?

If your answer is the latter, then I suggest you put this book down now and take a while to examine your life. But if you suggest the former, then you would be right. The obvious answer is because it's a lot easier to stop something before it has built up any momentum. Once any object has gained speed, direction and velocity, stopping it becomes a whole new level of difficult.

The same applies to whatever challenge you undertake. It's a far simpler task to back of out giving that speech when you're sitting in your seat. When you're walking up to the stage, it's a lot harder to quit. Avoiding that tandem skydive is a lot easier when you're on the ground than in the plane. Abandoning the hike up a hill is much more convenient when you're in the pub the night before than 100 metres from the summit.

The secret is building momentum quickly: the more momentum you have, the harder it is to embrace failure. That's all well and good, but how do you build momentum?

- **Start**: Yes, I know it sounds simple. But as someone who was trapped in their comfort zone for years, I know how cripplingly hard this can be. Every journey starts with a first step. And, by now, I'm way past all the decision-making, organisation and the rest of the dilly-dallying mentioned earlier in the book, which – while vital to the journey to your conquer zone – won't get you there alone. Whatever challenge you have chosen, there will be a point eventually when you have to put your grown-up pants on, take a deep breath, and walk through that fucking door even though you feel like getting into bed and hiding under the covers.
- **Small steps**: Relax, no one is expecting you to achieve glory in your first few steps, and if they are, you should get new friends. Momentum isn't about smashing all your goals. It's about taking small steps in the right direction. In those terrifying, early days when I was trying to discover how I was going to transform myself from a borderline alcoholic who

was surgically attached to the sofa into a competitor in the world's toughest footrace, I didn't think too much about goals or stats at all. The early victories for me were just getting out that door and doing something. Maybe it was 5k, maybe it was 10k or maybe it was staggering the four miles home from the pub instead of getting a taxi. The distance wasn't important. What mattered was that I had started to do *something*.

- **Continuing**: Once you have started doing something towards your goal – no matter how small – on a regular basis, it is vitally important to continue. It's all about momentum and progress. We naturally think progress towards our goals is a straight line in the right direction. It is anything but that. Whether you run around the same block, walk up the same hill or practice the same speech in your underwear each night, the key is to *keep doing it*. Every single day. Earlier on, we talked about how dangerous a train can be once it builds up some momentum, but it's devilishly easy for the driver to take their foot off the pedal, and what was once a speeding bullet can transform quickly back into an immobile lump of slowly rusting junk. Momentum cannot be sustained without continuing along the same path.

- **Ignore the diversions:** Life would be wonderful if the path to our goals and dreams was smooth, but life can be a bitch sometimes, so it's best to learn this quickly. I'm not going to get all Rambo here and tell you to ignore the haters, but it's best to remind yourself nice and early that nothing worth having was ever easy. In my training for the Marathon des Sables, so many obstacles were put in my way. I had friends and loved-ones telling me I was going to fail, fall apart or die. I suffered injuries ranging from a broken toe to a torn hamstring via a scratched eyeball. I had to drag myself out for training runs during one of the wettest and coldest winters in living memory. I even had to prepare for the heat by hanging around my local men's sauna at 10pm on Friday night, unaware that this time had been christened 'deflower hour' (don't ask). When these diversions confront you, it would be so easy to consider them a sign to stop. Fuck that. Instead, remind yourself that they are an indicator of you being on the right path to fulfilling your potential. This is just your comfort zone throwing excuses in your way desperately, and begging you to accept one and return to your unhappy existence. Whatever shit is thrown at you, smile and move past it. Because getting things you've never had means doing shit you've never, ever done.

Remember, your momentum doesn't have to be perfect and laser focused, you just need to be going in the right direction and shutting down those tantalising, seducing reasons to stop. My path through the desert on that fateful night wasn't perfectly straight and true, and it certainly involved its fair share of fuck-ups. But every step I took brought me closer to the general direction of my goal, and each metre took me further away from failure. By the time I was only a few miles away from the day's finish line, I couldn't have quit even if I wanted to (and, at times, I *really* did).

But you do need to be aware that your momentum needs *some* kind of purpose and direction. Without this, you risk fluttering around your conquer zone like a moth round a lightbulb – always so close to the light but forever getting burned.

This means that to get the benefit of momentum, you need to…

2. AVOID BEING A BUSY FOOL

Failure hangs around with busy fools.

Momentum is a powerful force, but it needs to be directed properly. Without direction, you can put in as much effort as you can possibly muster, but all it will do is help you to fail faster.

Throughout my corporate career, whenever I met a colleague and asked them how they were, without thinking, they would reply, "Busy". 'Busy' has become a badge of honour in our society, as if doing something – anything – is enough to make our dreams come true.

Busy is not a shield against poor preparation, half-hearted execution or unexpected events; it only allows us to pretend to ourselves that we are leaving our comfort zones. The reality, however, is that we are progressing no further towards conquering our goals, and we are giving ourselves an extra helping of stress at the same time.

In the run-up to the Marathon des Sables and in the race itself, competitors would obsess endlessly over trivial details, while telling themselves they were busy preparing for the race. As we have seen, preparation and organisation are absolutely vital to success, no matter the challenge we are trying to overcome, but this energy must be focused in the right way. I saw examples of my fellow racers obsessing for hours over the right kind of sunscreen to take, the correct laces for their shoes, or whether to wear a white or blue hat. In the quiet periods when we were camped amongst the sand dunes, roasted slowly by the sun like prawns on a barbeque, racers would – unbelievably – go for jogs or find rocks to lift in some bizarre, Flintstones-esque, Stone Age gym.

However, when I looked across to the tents of the elite racers – the Olympians and the seasoned, professional ultrarunners – there was only one thing they were doing: nothing. They were lying in the shade, quietly confident in their skills and preparations, conserving their energy for when they would need to perform. They had no need to show off, boast about how busy they were, or waste precious time and effort undertaking meaningless tasks; they waited like a pride of lions, preparing themselves silently for when the moment came to launch into action.

Like a lion, the prospect of failure can strike when we least expect it. We can put ourselves in a much better position to react and respond if we are prepared and ready, not exhausted from hours or days dithering and messing about. When I confronted failure on that night under the desert stars, no number of hours deliberating about laces, the brand of my sunscreen or the colour of my hat would have made a blind bit of difference. That time would have been better spent preparing my body and mind for the moment when I would need to call upon every piece of courage and strength I had.

You too can avoid being a busy fool by asking yourself a number of questions as you prepare for your challenge:

- *How will this activity impact my outcome?* If it doesn't have a direct impact on your success, you shouldn't be spending too much time on it.
- *If I need to do this activity, how can I complete it in the quickest and most efficient way possible?* No one over the age of 11 gets a certificate for hard work without outcomes. If you must do the activity, work out how to do it in the most efficient way possible to stop it diverting too much time. There are plenty of forums, groups and experts to consult – even people who will gladly accept your money to complete the task for you. After you decide to invest your time in doing something, invest wisely to get the best outcome in the quickest way.
- *How can I just focus on myself?* In any kind of group activity, such as the Marathon des Sables, a 10k race or a group hike, you will find a lot of people preparing independently to conquer the same goal. This is where 'exam syndrome' comes in. People will gather like teenagers before an exam, asking each other nervously, "How much work have you done?" and "What did you focus on?" The only reason this happens is because we want to make ourselves feel better by telling ourselves that we are the same as everyone else. All it achieves is making us feel terrible because we then feel underprepared compared to our peers.
- Shut out the noise, ignore the preparations and activities of other people (who are no wiser than you), and focus on only what will get you closer to your goals.

It is worth mentioning the theory of micro-improvements (otherwise known as marginal gains). This is often showcased by the efforts of Sir Dave Brailsford and the Great British Cycling team, who enjoyed unprecedented success by focusing on making tiny changes to seemingly insignificant things – handwashing, the thickness of cycling shorts, and the brightness levels in athlete's bedrooms – which added up to massive performance gains.[39] These miniscule improvements worked – and were absolutely not a waste of time – because they related directly to the challenges the team were trying to conquer. There is no shame in being busy and spending hours obsessing over tiny details if these will help you achieve your goal. But when you are 'busy' watching a six-hour Netflix documentary about Arnold Schwarzenegger instead of taking yourself to the gym, then the only thing you are getting closer to is your dreams going up in smoke before you can say *hasta la vista*.

Remember, stepping into your conquer zone while avoiding failure takes a tremendous amount of effort, but the only place *undirected* effort will get you to is back in your comfort zone.

3. ACCEPTING AN OUTSTRETCHED HAND

Like it or not, a time will come when we all need a little help to reach our goals. Just because our goals belong to us, and our journeys are something we must undertake alone, doesn't mean we can't accept a few helping hands along the way.

Sometimes, no matter whether or not that support is offered with the very best of intentions, it can still be difficult to accept. When I was first aware of Cameron's presence in the middle of that desert night, I wasn't the most welcoming of companions. I was cold, tired, injured and pissed off. The last thing I wanted was a Welshman whispering words of encouragement into my ear. It was only after the race that I realised that, although this might not have been what I wanted, it was exactly what I *needed* at that point in my journey.

In a time when we are encouraged to be more self-centred, suspicious and selfish than ever, helping others or accepting help can feel like the strangest thing we can imagine. You don't believe me? Jump on board any carriage on the Tube in London and start asking a

---

39   (2015). Viewpoint: Should we all be looking for marginal gains? *BBC News*. https://www.bbc.co.uk/news/magazine-34247629

stranger if there is anything you can do to help them achieve their life goals. See what reaction you get.

History is littered with examples of proud failures who refused to ask for help and slapped away the hands of assistance when they were offered. On a similar note, none of our greatest achievements were made by one person on their own. Neil Armstrong had Buzz and Adrian backing him up, supported by a cast of thousands of scientists, engineers and mathematicians. For her advances in the identification and treatment of cancer, Marie Curie was the first woman to win a Nobel Prize (and the first *person* to win the honour twice), and she raised a small fortune in the US and Europe to help fund new laboratories. She didn't, however, consider it a failure if other researchers and scientists stepped in to support and advance her work. It was she who had taken those brave first steps into the world of medical physics, and she who had made the groundbreaking, humanity-changing discoveries, but it is also thanks to other doctors, nurses, technicians, researchers and fundraisers that this work saves so many lives today.

So, when you're trying to step into your conquer zone and someone offers you support, remember:

- **It's not cheating:** Nowhere is it written in stone that you can't accept help. Once you have achieved your goals, no one will turn around and say, "Yeah, but you didn't really do it because so-and-so helped you." Getting support is human, and if you really want to step out of your comfort zone, it's natural to get help. After all, if you're doing something you've never done before, you're much more likely to succeed with the help of others who can show you the way.

- **You're not failing:** Getting help does not mean failure. Accepting an offer of assistance means you know yourself, and your strengths and weaknesses. It also means you recognise that you could do with a helping hand. The quickest way to embrace failure and comfort is to think you can go it alone and are above getting help. Alternatively, if you refuse assistance when, deep down, you know you really need it, you are setting yourself up for a fall. Refusing to accept help means you are embracing fear: fear of being vulnerable and fear of admitting you don't have all the answers. As we know, fear that is not addressed leads to suffering at worst, and a life stuck in your comfort zone wondering, *What if?* at best.

- **You're helping someone else:** Never underestimate how, by accepting the offer of support, you are actually helping the *other person*. When someone steps in to lend a hand, it's natural for our comfort zone to roll its eyes and tell us, "This person is only helping you because they think you're too weak/stupid/ foolish to succeed on your own." Think about it another way: maybe this person has come into your life at exactly the right time because it's part of their journey to help *you*. Don't take it so personally. Maybe this person has been helped by others in the past and wants to pay it forwards. Perhaps they are trying to make up for missed opportunities in their own lives. Maybe they know how good it feels to help someone else instead of just walking on by. Your journey to your conquer zone is your own, but it doesn't mean that your path won't cross with others every once in a while.

- **The victory is still yours:** Getting support shouldn't make your journey any less unique or successful. As we saw previously regarding the amazing achievements of Marie Curie and Neil Armstrong, they received so much help before, during and after their endeavours, but they will always be remembered for being the people who stepped forwards and chose to do something different. The same goes for you. This doesn't mean that help should not be remembered, acknowledged and recognised – quite the opposite, in fact. But it also means that support should not dilute the achievements you have made or will make. So, when that helping hand comes your way, accept and embrace it. The journey into your conquer zone is lonely enough at times, so there is no need to foolishly go it alone for the sake of it.

4. FAITH

As I experienced on that lonely night in the desert, there are times when all the momentum and all the support in the world are not enough. Sometimes life smacks our arses, and there's nothing we can do about it.

At times like this, we must dig deep and have faith that it's all going to be OK. I don't mean faith in the religious sense (but if it helps to pray to whatever god you follow, then, by all means, knock yourself out), I mean in another way: faith is the complete confidence and trust in someone or something.

In this case, that 'someone' is you, and that 'something' is your ability to step into your conquer zone. When all else had failed me under a billion stars in the Sahara Desert, when not even Cameron's encouraging words could spur me forwards and stop me worrying about my disorientation and blood-pissing, all I had left was the ability to tell myself that *it was going to be OK.*

Because sometimes life deals us a shitty hand. Then another. Then it knocks us down and pisses on us. We all have points when we are on our knees, looking skywards, and asking, *"Really? Have you not given me enough problems to deal with?"*

This is when we must dig deep into our conquer zone and develop a bulletproof mindset. This isn't about being the toughest, the most unstoppable or any of that macho bullshit; it's about having the quiet confidence that everything is going to be OK. You might not have all the answers, or the vision or plan for how you're going to get yourself out of this mess, but what you do have is the ability to tell yourself it will all work out.

Maybe it won't happen today, tomorrow or even in six months. Perhaps it won't work out the way you planned, but it *will* get better. And the ability to dig deep down into your heart and remind yourself of this when it seems like the whole universe is against you, and when it feels like total, abject failure is only a heartbeat away – this is faith.

I couldn't see it at the time, but when my father decided to poison himself with years of alcohol abuse and then decided to die, followed by my own personal descent into mental illness, struggles with alcohol and losing the career I had sacrificed so much for, it all happened for a reason.

If that series of unfortunate events hadn't have happened, I wouldn't be in the position I found myself in: struggling against the odds, staring failure in the face and staggering over the finish line of day four, 56 miles and 22 hours after I had started.

Without momentum, continuous small steps, a lot of help from Cameron and a little bit of faith, my journey into my conquer zone might have ended forever in that lost, soul-destroying night in the desert.

*

The early rays of the sun heralded the arrival of fat, greedy flies landing on my face. I shuffled in my sleeping bag and took a peek at my watch: 6.32am. I'd only slept for a couple of hours. Casting my mind back to the events of the previous day and evening, it all felt like a strange nightmare. I still wasn't able to get my head around how close to failure – and serious injury – I'd come.

As I unravelled myself from my cocoon, I winced as I slipped on my battered trainers and heaved myself to my feet. Almost immediately, I was overcome by dizziness and the urge to vomit, and my hand moved instinctively to support the small of my back, where it felt as if someone had given me the good news with a baseball bat. It was time to get some medical attention.

Around 100 agonising yards away stood the medical tent. It was a makeshift field hospital manned by a team of volunteer doctors, catering for a steady flow of walking wounded competitors, who were complaining of everything from diarrhoea, blisters and sprained ankles to scorpion stings and head injuries.

The French doctor smiled as I approached slowly, shuffling like an old man who had just undergone a hip replacement. "Ah, it is you. We thought you would be here by now."

"*Moi*? Why? Were you expecting me?" Once again, I adopted the very British approach of not even trying to speak the man's native language.

"We watched you cross the finish line in the early hours. You were in a lot of trouble, no? We thought you would not make it."

"Me neither, mate; I thought it was game over for me. To be honest with you, I don't know if I can carry on."

The doctor gave a very French shrug. "*Bof*, you will fine. You're still breathing, no? Monsieur, if you are still breathing, then you are *still in the race!*"

I tried to muster a faint smile and hoped he was right. I knew I had to somehow pull my mind and body together to run one more marathon through the sand in just a few hours' time. I knew I was going to need all the help I could get.

Suddenly, a thought occurred to me: *Cameron could help!* I knew I couldn't have made it through the previous night without his constant encouragement and support. Although I hardly knew the man, I wanted his hulking mass by my side more than ever. But I didn't know which tent he was in. In my distress, I hadn't even caught a glimpse of his race number.

"Er… *monsieur*?" I asked the doctor tentatively, "When you saw me cross the finish line early this morning, there was a man who was with me; do you know what his race number was? Or did you happen to see which tent he went into?"

A blank expression crossed the doctors face. "A man? There was no man with you, *monsieur*."

I was confused. "You could hardly miss him, mate. He was about 10 feet tall; a big, Welsh guy."

"*Non, monsieur*," the doctor repeated. "I remember it very clearly because you were quite distressed."

It felt suddenly as if a winter breeze had blown into the medical tent. I shivered involuntarily as a nagging truth began to creep into my bones. "There… there must be… You must be mistaken. There *was* a man; he helped me through the desert."

"Sir, there is no mistake." The doctor looked deep into my eyes and smiled. "You were only helped by yourself. Last night… you crossed the desert alone."

TWELVE

FINDING YOUR CONQUER ZONE

The time for motivational speeches was over.

I'd given everything I had to get through the darkness. The bank was now empty. I had no more energy and no more strength. The reserves of willpower and encouragement were drained.

The truth be told, I no longer cared about how I finished this race, and my reasons for entering in the first place had been long forgotten. All my proud – some might call it arrogant – words of "inspiring people to do the things they thought they couldn't do" had become a distant memory.

I just wanted to go home.

As 'Highway to Hell' blasted across the loudspeakers one more time, I struggled to raise my eyes from the sandy ground. The 56 miles I had covered the previous day had destroyed my strength, spirit and feet. The medic's words from earlier still made my head spin: *Had Cameron been a figment of my imagination all along? A hallucination created by my exhausted and dehydrated mind to tell me what I needed to hear in order to get through the night? Or had the doctor just been mistaken?*

I realised I could tie my mind in knots trying to work out this problem, but it didn't really matter. All that counted was the here and now, the hours that lay ahead, and the sand, mountains, parched riverbeds and treacherous valleys that stood between me and a finisher's medal.

A shove in the back snapped me from my thoughts. I hadn't even realised that the crowd of athletes in front of me had started to surge forward. With a grunt and a grimace, I picked up my feet. It was time to see whether the months of training, setbacks, arguments, worries and injuries had been enough. Today was the day it mattered the most – it was time to embrace my conquer zone, or to fall at the final hurdle and subject myself to a lifetime of *maybes* and *what-ifs*.

Welcome to the final day of the Marathon des Sables.

*

Have you ever built something up *so* much that it feels like a slight let-down when it actually happens?

In my mind, I had always seen myself galloping over sand dunes and running freely across the arid wilderness with a smile on my face, and with the cheers from local Bedouin tribespeople greeting my ears as I advanced on the finish line like a slightly sunburned Lawrence of Arabia. After everything I'd been through before and during the race, I imagined the final day would be a breeze.

The desert had other ideas. It wasn't going to let me go without a fight.

Storm-force winds blasted sand into my eyes and mouth as I staggered forward, almost bent double against its intensity. Another nagging injury I had picked up days earlier was starting to sound the alarm: the left strap of my backpack had been pressing continually against the top of my shoulder and a nerve in the base of my neck was now alight. Any sideways movement of my head sent a torrent of pain shooting from my skull down to the base of my spine.

I tried to look on the bright side: I hadn't pissed blood for a whole six hours.

It's strange: The closer we get to victory, the more all we can think of is defeat. At this late stage, I still doubted my ability to finish the race. I struggled to think about all the achievements that had brought me to this point, and I could only see the perils in my path. I started to daydream about how it would feel to collapse within sight of the finish line, what I would say to my children and fundraisers if I failed, and whether I could ever muster the courage to return to this beautiful, destructive land and finish the job.

Another blast of wind forced my head sideways like a backstreet chiropractor and I was rewarded with another jolt of pain. I tried to use this to snap out of my mindset, realising I was in danger of feeling very sorry for myself.

Clambering gingerly up the crumbling, six-foot-high wall of earth that was once the bank of a long-evaporated river, I considered my own climbs and struggles to reach this point. A burst of insight hit me unexpectedly: I was no longer scared of failure.

The fear of failure that had stalked me for years had been abandoned in the sand, days before. Although the last thing I wanted to do was fail or disappoint my supporters, I was no longer scared by it. I had come so far, worked so hard, and transformed my body and mind into something stronger than I could ever have imagined, but if I was not good enough on this final day, then so be it.

With surprising clarity, I understood suddenly. *This* was the final threshold we must cross to enter our conquer zone: totally and utterly losing our fear of failure. Crawling through the dust, I realised that to achieve our goals finally, we cannot crowd our minds with nightmares, disasters or negative occurrences that may or may not happen. We must give ourselves to our challenge with the quiet confidence that we will succeed, and the certain belief that if we falter and fail, we absolutely will rise again and be a better person for the experience.

This realisation brought another revelation: the thing I was truly terrified by was actually *success*.

YOU ARE GOOD ENOUGH

Daydreaming is so much easier than action. It allows our comfort zones to make our lives all the more pleasant without having to go through the effort, risk and fear of seeing if we are truly capable of making those dreams come true.

It's easy – and common – to not try to do something because we fear failure. Too often, our minds are conditioned to think about the negative consequences and what can go wrong, but there is a deeper, darker truth.

It's no different to approaching a long-term crush nervously and finally asking them out on a date. You have spent days and weeks building up the courage, and you are certain they will laugh and turn you down, but the thought of them saying yes is an equally, if not more, terrifying prospect.

We fear success because so many of us have told ourselves a story for so long. This is a story of *not being good enough*. While this story isn't pleasant, it serves the purpose of keeping us nice and safe in our comfort zones and never having to do anything extraordinary, while not risking embarrassing or spectacular failure. Believing we are not good enough is a fast-pass to the front of the line for a solidly unspectacular 5/10 life.

But what if you started to believe you *are* good enough? Now that is a truly terrifying prospect. Suddenly, all the stories you told yourself, all the patterns, all the routines, the relationships, the plans and the processes – everything – can be shifted. Nothing is as it was.

Once you realise that you don't have to limit yourself with your old beliefs any more, a whole scary, new world of opportunity opens before you. You realise that you don't have to stick with the same job, relationship, country, friendship group or hobby if you don't want to. Anyone who has ever had a puppy or kitten will know that you keep them in one room of the house at first to allow them to get comfortable and settled. They get used to their environment and start to relax. Then, when you leave the door open and allow them to explore the rest of the house, they become timid and scared. The animal does not want to leave familiarity and comfort, even though a much more exciting and fulfilling world of adventure awaits.

As I started slowly to cover the miles of sand on my final day across that Martian landscape, I didn't become more excited about the prospect of victory. The intense feeling of fear started to build up inside me, like a boiling pot on a stove, threatening to bubble over at any point.

I thought back to all those hours spent in bars with my friends when, drink in hand, I'd mentioned this crazy idea about running through the Sahara Desert. As they ridiculed my hopes and dreams, and made jokes such as, "You'll have to carry a litre of vodka on your back and hitch a ride on a camel," I would laugh along as well.

This was all part of the story I had told myself and the persona I had created. I was the party guy. The guy who would always buy you a drink. The guy who would laugh at himself. The person who was great fun to have on a night out, but who you would never want to work with or entrust anything important to. The guy who never took anything seriously – including himself. The guy who went with you to the bar when he wanted to go to the gym. The guy who nodded when you said you wanted pizza, but he really wanted salad. The guy you took to the nightclub on a Tuesday night when he had work to do. The guy who once drank a cup of piss because you thought it would be funny. The guy who wanted desperately to be accepted by everyone, and who was so eager to please that he would put his own happiness and self-worth on the back burner.

I liked that guy. I knew where I stood with him. I knew what he preferred and what he was capable of. I knew absolutely all of his limits, and I knew not to push them.

And now I was going to kill him.

Sometimes we must destroy the things we love, even if it's the last thing we want to do. Sometimes the grassland needs to burn for new shoots of life to grow.

By taking a different path, by deciding to turn towards success rather than failure, and by choosing to step into my conquer zone finally instead of opting for an easier life of comfort, excuses and failed promises, I was destroying the old version of myself and becoming the person I knew I could be.

As terrifying as it seemed, it was time to tell myself a different story. I wasn't perfect – far from it – nor would I ever be. But I had somehow managed to create a stupid, crazy, ambitious goal, and then develop the discipline and motivation to get myself to the start line of the world's toughest footrace. Now, as the finish line got nearer, no one was more surprised than me to discover that I did actually have what it takes.

I was good enough.

BURYING THE PAST

The scenery was changing.

I tried to glance at my surroundings without moving my head and triggering another blinding shot of pain through my neck. The dry, desolate landscape was finally starting to show signs of life. Motorcycle tracks criss-crossed the sand beneath my feet. On the horizon, an unfamiliar sight greeted my eyes: green trees. I had become accustomed to seeing nothing but different shades of yellow and beige, so much so that the fresh vegetation struck me as looking as peculiar as this desert had only a week ago.

To my left, the ground rose upwards to form a small ridge. Atop the slope was a collection of burned ruins; the blackened and scarred stones formed the skeletons of shacks and outcrops from hundreds of years ago. I wondered absently what the long-deceased inhabitants would think of this collection of foreigners running through their land and paying for the privilege. Would they salute our achievements of travelling unthinkable distances in unimaginable conditions? Or would they look on in disbelief as they fought a daily battle to survive in such a harsh environment, wondering why these rich travellers would voluntarily leave a life of gilded comfort in order to make their existences more difficult and traumatic than they needed to be?

The heat seemed to radiate from this rubble, reminding me it was early afternoon and the temperature would be reaching its daily high of 50 degrees Celsius. As if on cue, a giant camel spider the size of my hand pattered in front me and scampered for shelter under a shrub.

Rounding the corner of a rocky outcrop, I saw a huge, flat plain stretching out before me. Its orange, sandy surface was pock-marked by a million black rocks, each the size of a grapefruit, as if a firestorm of meteorites had fallen from the sapphire heavens. What really caught my attention, however, were the specks of activity in the distance.

A cluster of shapes stood on the horizon, no more than a collection of colours shimmering in the heat haze. My ears picked up the faint sounds of rotors as I observed two helicopters buzzing above the site like tiny birds of prey. Stretching between this strange outpost of activity and me was a thin line of athletes, spread out as if they were a colony of hungry ants heading towards their nest.

The finish line.

Everything I'd hoped for, everything I'd worked towards and the goal so many people said was impossible was right there in front of me. Even more importantly, an ice-cold drink and fresh underwear were within touching distance.

The only problem was that I didn't want it.

My shuffling run slowed to a walk, then, finally, I stopped, confused, like a supermarket shopper who couldn't remember where they parked the car. Athletes raced past me, giving me quizzical, sideways looks. They slowed to ask why I wasn't sprinting towards my goal and why I was not reaching out to grab the victory being presented to me.

One woman stopped alongside me, perhaps – I guessed – to offer some assistance. Instead, she simply pulled down her shorts, squatted and pissed. Without a word, she gave herself a wiggle, pulled up her garments and continued on her way to victory.

It's strange, I thought, *how humans love a life of comfort so much, yet so quickly become comfortable with the most uncomfortable of things.*

A solitary tear welled in my eye and formed a clean river through a week's worth of sand and dust as it travelled down my cheek. I thought back to my father, lying on his deathbed, and whether he had been happy with what he had accomplished. I asked him silently if he had any regrets, and if he was proud of me for trying to finally live my life like there could be no tomorrow.

But, at that moment, I realised I had been wrong. I *couldn't* live and act like there could be no tomorrow. I had to do the things that would make my children proud, and their children too. I wanted to be remembered by distant generations, not for doing crazy, stupid, extreme shit, but for living a life that made *me* proud. I knew I wouldn't always succeed; I knew I would rarely – if ever – be the best, but I could be known for *giving my best*, for making my dreams come true and for never limiting myself. I could lead by example and leave a legacy of being the person who never wanted to stay within his comfort zone for too long.

"I have to say goodbye to you now," my voice was choked with emotion as I spoke to my father. "You'll always be a part of my past, but I can no longer use you as an excuse for not creating my future. Now I'm going to finish this race. For me."

I picked up my feet, and left my fear of success, my fear of failure, and my fear of every damn person and their thoughts, words and opinions in the dust.

Running faster than I had in days, I sprinted towards the finish line. All thoughts, worries and complexities emptied from my mind. I smiled as I tried to savour the moment, wanting this achievement more than anything before in my life, while trying to treasure every detail at the same time because I knew it would gone in a second.

I threw myself across the finish line like a drowning man lunges at a rope. Overcome with emotion, I dropped to my knees and threw my fists into the air in victory. A guttural roar exploded from my lungs. It was a scream against the old version of me; all the doubters who had tried to dissuade me; the desert that had tried to kill me; and my comfort zone – which had tried every trick in the book to stop me making my dreams come true.

As the race organiser and original desert explorer, Patrick Bauer, hugged me and placed my medal around my neck, I kissed the cool metal and smiled up at the sky.

I had found my conquer zone.

THIRTEEN

CONQUERING YOUR FUTURE

Sitting on my arse had never felt so good.

I steadied myself, took a breath, and used every ounce of strength and focus to reach out for my intended target. And I grabbed it. I managed to clutch the TV remote control without upsetting the delicate balance of two children, a cat and a pizza box, which were all sitting precariously on my lap.

The four weeks since I'd arrived back from the Sahara Desert had been a blur of visits, presentations and press interviews, plus trips to the local takeaway. My toenails had grown back, my kidneys had stopped pissing blood, my weight had returned, and I'd finally stopped finding sand in the shower.

Life was comfortable.

It was amazing how quickly someone could slip from being on the edge of madness and in the epicentre of their conquer zone to being entrapped back in a wonderful land of comfort. As I absently watched a nature documentary about polar bears while trying to cram another slice of mighty-meatball pizza into my mouth, my oldest son nuzzled into me.

"Daddy? I was wondering if I could be like you one day..." he said.

I smiled as my chest swelled with pride. Finally, by stepping into my conquer zone, I'd become the man my children could be proud of. "You know, my boy, I'm so happy to hear you say—"

He cut me off. "But, actually, I *don't* want to be like you."

My ego deflated like a punctured tyre.

He went on, "I don't want to go into my canker zone when I grow up. I want to paint pictures and do crafts and make things… I think."

"It's *conquer* zone," I corrected him for the hundredth time. "But that's what the conquer zone is all about… It's not doing these crazy, extreme things I do. I only do these things because they are *my* goals."

He nodded, still unsure of what I meant.

"You see," I continued, trying not choke on my pizza crust. "Everyone has a conquer zone, and it's not about what I want, or Mummy or your friends… Your conquer zone is about *your* passions and goals. Your conquer zone is a precious place, so don't waste it on living someone else's dreams. Keep it just for you."

"Oh, OK. I'll do that then," he replied.

I smiled to myself; if only adults could decide to follow their passions so easily.

Something else stirred inside me, and it wasn't the full English breakfast I'd had that morning. I knew I was at a turning point. I could happily let my comfort zone take control, return to my old behaviours and routines, settle back into a not-totally-unhappy-but-unfulfilled existence. After all, the desert had given me a lifetime's worth of stories to dine out on. I had a sudden premonition of a 50-year-old version of myself, bloated and arrogant, still making the same old excuses and still allowing my comfort zone to win. I could be propping up some dusty bar, talking to anyone who would listen, slurring my words as I insisted I had *once* been someone capable of running through the Sahara Desert.

This could be the end or just the beginning. I could use my recent discovery of my conquer zone as a springboard to greater things: help more people and conquer new goals.

On the TV programme I was watching, two polar bears were

fighting, observed by a family of bored-looking wolves. The pack stood motionless as the snow fell around them; they were unflinching as the flakes blew into their large, dark, all-seeing eyes. They were waiting.

My pizza crust demolished, I reached for my phone. Something I'd seen online only the day before had sparked my attention once again.

I opened the webpage and devoured the content: "The world's coldest ultramarathon, 200 miles through the frozen Artic."

In that amazing way in which a child never misses a thing, my son's attention was captured. "Daddy, are you thinking of going running with the polar bears?"

"I think I'm tempted," I replied, my finger already reaching for the 'confirm' button. "Do you think I could do it?"

He snuggled in and squeezed me tightly, his dozing eyes once again focused on the polar bear battle unfurling on the TV. "Of course you can do it, Daddy. You can do anything you want… just step into your canker zone."

THE END

But really, it's just the beginning

Thank you for being a part of this wonderful adventure.

Anything is possible, if you have the burning desire to make it happen. So now, it's your turn.

I'd love to hear what you have in store.

You can follow me on Instagram @FreddieExplores and email me at hello@freddiembennett.com

Now put this book down, and go and make it happen.

After all, it's about time.